Go the Distance provide~ ___ ____ ___ ___ ___ p___ __ success. It is a "must" for anyone seeking practical ways to become a true winner in life. Ed Rowell's explanations of the keys to being a true winner are clear and concise and his blending of timeless truth and practical real life stories make it a joy to read.

—E. K. Bailey
Pastor, Concord Church
President, E. K. Bailey Ministries, Inc.

Two tasks on my to-do list this week were to read Ed Rowell's manuscript of *Go the Distance* and review my retirement program, which is due to be activated in ten years. Reading Ed's book has been more helpful in preparing me to finish my career with strength than meeting with my financial advisor to readjust my depleted investments. Mixing good biblical studies with the wisdom of Jesus and Ben Franklin, and flavored with a healthy dose of humor and practical advice, Ed Rowell has produced an outstanding handbook for the Christian leader who wants to "go the distance." Minister and layperson alike will profit from the twenty-one topics discussed as they see themselves challenged and mirrored in the characters from Ed Rowell's personal experience and research. Before planning retirement, every baby boomer should read *Go the Distance* and follow Ed's model for effective guidance in leadership and service.

—Jerry B. Cain, President
Judson College, Elgin, Illinois

Ed Rowell has clearly defined the characteristics, attributes, and actions of a winner! *Go the Distance* is an excellent book for those who are determined to win in the game of *life*.

I would recommend this book to anyone who wants to develop a strategy and form the habits necessary to *win!*

—Karen B. Ford
Independent National Sales Director

I've observed Ed Rowell as a rodeo contestant, a preacher, a writer, an editor, and an interviewer. He's a keen observer and a great storytells who has a gift of quickly connecting with people. As you read *Go the Distance*, you'll see that this book, like Ed himself, will leave you encouraged.

—Marshall Shelley, Vice President
Christianity Today International

GO THE

DISTANCE

GO THE

21 HABITS & ATTITUDES FOR WINNING AT LIFE

DISTANCE

ED ROWELL

BROADMAN
&HOLMAN
PUBLISHERS

NASHVILLE, TENNESSEE

Published by Broadman & Holman Publishers, Nashville, Tennessee

Dewey Decimal Classification: 248
Subject Heading: CHRISTIAN LIVING

Unless otherwise noted, Scripture quotations are from the Holy Bible, New International Version, copyright © 1973, 1978, 1984 by International Bible Society. Other versions are identified by acronym, as follows: KJV, King James Version. NKJV, New King James Version, copyright © 1979, 1980, 1982, Thomas Nelson, Inc., Publishers. NRSV, New Revised Standard Version of the Bible, copyright © 1989 by the Division of Christian Education of the National Council of Churches of Christ in the United States of America, used by permission, all rights reserved. RSV, Revised Standard Version of the Bible, copyrighted 1946, 1952, © 1971, 1973. NLT, New Living Translation, copyright © 1996. Used by permission of Tyndale House Publishers, Inc., Wheaton, Illinois 60189. All rights reserved.

Throughout this book I tell stories about people I've met in researching this topic. Because of the personal nature of these stories, many names and identifying details have been changed to protect their privacy. In the case of stories that happened to me, I have also changed identifying details in some cases to protect the confidentiality of my relationship with parishioners both present and past. If you recognize yourself in one of these illustrations, rest assured it wasn't you I was talking about.

Library of Congress Cataloging-in-Publication Data

Rowell, Edward K.
  Go the distance : 21 habits & attitudes for winning at life / Ed Rowell.
      p.   cm.
  Includes bibliographical references.
  ISBN 0–8054–2150–5 (pb.)
  1. Success—Religious aspects—Christianity. I. Title.

BV4598.3 .R69 2002
248.4—dc21
                                                              2001043996

Dedication

WHILE I WAS WORKING ON THIS BOOK, I frequently thought of two men, my teachers, both of whom died unexpectedly. Both had a profound influence on my life and, ultimately, this book.

Dick Dunagan was my sixth-grade teacher. Mr. D. invested in me both as a lonely boy who needed some attention, and later as a young man who needed some direction. In the classroom he taught me to love literature and gave me my first encouragement as a writer. I wrote a story about a cowboy who had to shoot his horse. When I got the graded story back, there was a note at the top.

"Eddie—

This almost made me cry. A+.

Mr. D."

His involvement in my life didn't stop in class. On his farm he taught me to ride a horse well, drive a tractor, trap coyotes, bail hay, deliver calves, and keep my word no matter what the cost. Following a painful event in early adulthood, I moved to be near Dick and his wife, Mary Ellen. They loved me through a time when I felt most unlovable and kept me from self-destructing.

I loved Mr. D. deeply and regret never telling him so.

Ed Trotter was my high-school science teacher and coach. No one before or after has pushed me to excel like Mr. Trotter did. Whether in the classroom or on the athletic field, he could motivate me like no one else. I was both scared to death of him and also desperate to win his approval. I remember a track practice in early spring. As darkness crept up on us, I turned in my best time of the season for the quarter mile, trying to win the right to anchor our mile relay team. When I crossed the finish line, I caught the slightest glimmer of satisfaction as he looked at his stopwatch. He never said a word, but I knew he was pleased. I lived on that affirmation for weeks.

The summer after I graduated I was shocked to discover his gruff exterior was like a suit of clothes. He put it on for his students and took it off for his friends. I was proud to graduate from student to friend.

For years after I left my hometown of Reserve, New Mexico, when I accomplished anything of significance (college and seminary graduation, marriage, first published article), I would tell Mom over the phone, "Be sure and tell Mr. Trotter about me."

I'd look him up when I went back for a visit. "I always knew you'd make a difference in this world," he'd say. I believed him when he said it.

The death of both these teachers grieved me deeply. But the loss reminded me of the incredible power of believing in someone. Without a doubt, they had an impact on hundreds of other students they taught. I'm just glad they took time to invest in me.

This book is dedicated to these two men who made all the difference in my life.

Contents

Foreword

FOR THREE DAYS I have been carefully selecting material to put in my briefcase. The reason for such planning? I'm going to South Africa for a week. Knowing I will spend forty hours in airports and on planes, I want to have plenty of writing projects and reading material. The last material I put in my briefcase was this book . . . and I'm glad I did! Halfway through my flight I picked up *Go the Distance*. I never put it down until I finished it. Ed will be proud of me for "finishing well."

As I write this foreword several thoughts flood my mind. I enjoyed this book because . . .

- I love the theme. Ed is right on when he gives the following premise of the book: "Real success is the result of implementing simple disciplines and practicing them constantly over time." Amen and amen!
- I appreciate the simplicity. Ed is a communicator. He takes the complex, breaks it down, and applies truth to my life. I found myself continually identifying his writing to my journey.
- My personal "take-aways" were many. One of the ways I place value on a book is by counting the material that I mark and file for my personal filing and growth. A great book will provide twenty "take-aways" for me. This book had forty-four!
- The biblical application was excellent. The book never got off track. The content was within the framework of God's Word.

• I know the author. Ed Rowell and I have been friends for several years and we have many shared experiences. What he wrote in this book is how he lives. He practices the daily disciplines of a winner. Often I say in conferences, "We teach what we know, but we reproduce what we are." This book should produce many winners who develop a winning lifestyle!

Whenever I read a book that has been helpful to me, I quickly recommend it to others.

You can pick this book up with the assurance that it contains life-changing words for your life's journey. I heartily recommend it to you . . . and when I arrive in Capetown, I will recommend it to them. Turn these pages and discover the winner within you.

Dr. John C. Maxwell, Founder
The INJOY Group
www.INJOY.com

Preface

THE WORLD IN WHICH I LIVED as a child was quite small. I could walk to my elementary school. Our church and grocery store were within a few miles of our home. We took no vacations and seldom traveled farther than the seventy miles to my maternal grandparents' home. I knew little about the world beyond our town. When I was in fourth grade, my parents began a difficult physical and spiritual quest, searching for a better life for our family. We moved back and forth across the southwestern United States six times in the next five years. We finally settled in a little community in western New Mexico called Reserve, where I lived until the age of twenty-one. I suspect they settled down there as much out of weariness as from any sense of finding what they were looking for.

Those transient years wrought in me both the ability to adapt to change quickly and to embrace new opportunities before they escaped. For that I am grateful.

They also created in me an insatiable longing for stability and security. The result has been a restless relationship with the status quo. I simultaneously long to move beyond it, yet crave the solidity it provides.

As an adult, I have had to live in tension between these two desires. I have wanted to embrace every new opportunity and understanding, and yet hang on to what I already know. I want to move on to bigger and better places and experiences and adventures, yet not leave where I am or what I'm doing. In talking to others, I believe my experience is quite common in our culture.

For me, the greatest challenge has been finding my place in a world that is infinitely larger and more complex than I ever dreamed, and making a difference in that world in some way.

I want to succeed but not by the most common definition of the word. It is not fame and fortune I seek, not power or position. I can't deny that at times those goals have seemed alluring. But I've seen too many people attain them and still live a life of desperate searching.

This tension began for me a quest not unlike the one my parents took years ago, though mine has been more internal. It has centered around defining success, then identifying the roadblocks that were keeping me from reaching that success.

That's what this book is about. I hope it will spur you on to think through your own definition of success and what is keeping you from attaining it. If a few of these chapters speak to you, then I will have succeeded in helping a fellow traveler find his way home.

Ed Rowell
Franklin, Tennessee

The Difference Between Winning and Losing

*Life must be lived forward
but it can only be evaluated backward.*
—Søren Kierkegaard

OUTSIDE AN ELEMENTARY SCHOOL in a major city in Texas, most teachers sit in their cars each morning as long as possible, summoning the will and courage to walk into their classrooms for one more day. Once inside, they will wage a mostly losing battle against the legacy of poverty, ignorance, drugs, and hopelessness that defines the community surrounding this school.

Only 12 percent of their students have two parents in the home. Children barely old enough for puberty are having babies. Many arrive hungry, even though the school offers breakfast. Some went home the day before to an empty apartment; their mother was gone when they got home and still wasn't back when they left this morning. A few spent the whole night lying on the floor under their bed, crying, praying, barely dozing, while gunfire echoed in the streets.

If their home situations weren't reason enough to keep these children in bondage, the school board is corrupt and the teachers have grown weary of making bricks without straw. There are never enough books to go around. Broken desks outnumber working desks; children sit on the floor in most classrooms. Supplies for bulletin boards, art, and parties are already being paid for by the teacher, and the district is talking of cutting the budget even further.

While her colleagues sit in the parking lot, Myra Banks has already been in her classroom for an hour. Worship music flows from a small compact disc player as she places home-baked muffins on each desk and prays for the student who sits there.

Myra is a born teacher. Gifted. Almost forty years of experience. She could easily be teaching in the same suburban district where her own kids attended. Most of her teacher friends have either given up and left the vocation or found another district where their lives are no longer in danger.

But Myra won't quit. She can't. Even during the really hard days, something keeps her going. She has developed some habits and attitudes that allow her to press on in spite of the odds, in spite of the danger, in spite of the cost. Myra Banks is making a difference.

Meanwhile out in Orange County, California, Rob Baker is making lattes and mochas in an upscale coffee shop for minimum wage plus tips. Just over a year ago, he pulled the plug on his life's dream of planting a church that would reach unchurched people. Despite five years of hard work and fervent prayer, the church never really got on its feet. So he gave up. Quit. Walked away.

No one had prepared him for the toll that church-planting would take on his body and his spirit. Rob lives with tremendous guilt. He had, and still has, a strong sense that God called him to ministry. But this task was just too hard. He feels scarred, damaged, and doubts he'll ever step back into a ministry position.

His wife, Wendy, has a seventy-five-minute commute to her job at a major accounting firm. As she drives, she prays. She begs God to restore to her husband the passion, purpose, and urgency he once had for ministry. She wonders if he will ever overcome his scars, his pain, his utter sense of failure.

The night he told her he was quitting, she had reminded him of his ordination, when his father (also a pastor) had preached from Philippians 3:13–14: "Forgetting what is behind and straining toward what is ahead, I press on toward the goal to win the prize for which God has called me heavenward in Christ Jesus."

His response to that memory? None at all. It was as if his heart had suddenly hardened to both her and God. Admittedly, he had suffered a major loss. But why did this setback cause this promising young pastor to drop out of the race of life at just thirty-two years of age?

Perhaps it was, in part, because he had never developed the habits, the attitudes that would see him through the inevitable hardships of life and ministry.

Why do some people make it through life in one piece, with their family, their character, their faith, and their sense of self-worth intact? What makes some successful and others . . . well, not? How does a person who follows Christ even define success?

The premise of this book is that *real success is the result of implementing simple disciplines and practicing them consistently over time.* Failure is often nothing more than a few simple errors in judgment, repeated consistently over time. These disciplines lead to authentic success only when they are focused toward our God-given purpose. Those errors steer us away from that purpose. The net effect of our disciplines and our judgments will lead us to either achievement or failure.

Here's the question I've been asking of everyone I know for years now: How can we come to the end of our lives and know we've accomplished that thing or things for which God created us? The answer to that question is significant, because for me there is no other sufficient definition of success for the devoted follower of Christ.

For years I have respected Howard Hendricks. As of this writing, Dr. Hendricks is seventy-six and is still carrying a full load. He has had a profound influence on thousands of students through his teaching as a professor at Dallas Theological

Seminary. He's influenced hundreds of thousands through his books and conference speaking.

I've had the chance to meet him through my work on several occasions. In the fall of 2000, we were together at a conference in Atlanta, and he gave me an hour of his time. I shared with him my plans for this book.

He shared something I had heard him say before and forgotten. In his ongoing study of leadership, he had found that the Bible names about one hundred people you could list as leaders. Here's the tragedy: only about a third of them finished well.

For example, Solomon, the world's wisest man, didn't finish well. He disobeyed God in two areas. First, God had told the Israelites not to marry outside their own nation—not because of race, but because of religion. Solomon neglected God's directive and took not one but seven hundred wives and three hundred concubines. The Bible declares, "His wives led him astray. As Solomon grew old, his wives turned his heart after other gods, and his heart was not fully devoted to the LORD his God, as the heart of David his father had been" (1 Kings 11:3–4).

I find these to be among the most depressing words in Scripture. To have accomplished all Solomon had accomplished yet not finish well . . . . If it could happen to him, it could happen to me.

Almost two thousand years ago, an aging missionary named Paul wrote to his young protégé. "I have fought the good fight, I have finished the race, I have kept the faith. Now there is in store for me the crown of righteousness, which the Lord, the righteous Judge, will award to me on that day—and not only to me, but also to all who have longed for his appearing" (2 Tim. 4:7–8).

When I read this passage, I often note the loneliness evident between the lines. Paul was at the end of his ministry, the future was uncertain and, except for Luke, he was all alone. But these words in verses 7–8 bring another emotion to mind: Satisfaction.

How satisfying Paul's memories must have been as he reviewed his life and found it complete. Recalling the hardships on one hand, he measured his eternal reward on the other. As he scratched the parchment with his ink-stained quill, he gave us powerful metaphors for winning at life: Fighting the good fight. Finishing the race. Keeping the faith.

A recent auto race gives us a metaphor for losing the race. At the eighty-third running of the Indianapolis 500, Robby Gordon, with just one lap to go, didn't have enough gasoline to finish.

While the other lead drivers had taken a pit stop when the yellow caution flag went up following a crash by Mark Dismore, Gordon gambled that he could finish the final thirty-seven laps on one tank of fuel. With just a lap to go he had to pull in for a "splash" of methanol. The stop caused him to finish in fourth place.

Gordon shared rule number one in racing: "You must first finish before you finish first."[1] Gordon learned that lesson the hard way. The fuel gauge in his car had been warning him for some time, but he chose to postpone the solution. The stakes in our lives are much higher. As soon as the warning light goes off in one critical area of life, *that* is the time to make adjustments or course corrections. Otherwise, a poor finish could be our legacy.

How do we plan to run our race well, to finish well, when so many around us quit running when the first little cramp sets in? All of us will experience the inevitable pain of life. All of us will face hardships. All of us will suffer loss. All of us will encounter injustice and be disappointed by others. Life is hard. Life is not fair. All runners in this race face their own unique set of hurdles. Most of us will trip over some of them before we get to the end. Yet a few of us will get up and run again, eventually crossing the finish line triumphantly, while others will trip over that first hurdle and never get up out of the dirt.

I'm concerned about my own generation. As baby boomers move slowly but surely toward retirement, we're dropping out of life in droves. I see far too many people bailing out of their marriages. I have known too many of my colleagues who have bailed out of ministry. I've seen too many people lose their passion for work and begin either to coast or merely to survive until retirement.

I know too many Christians who are going through the motions of their faith, having lost the joy, hope, and peace that Christ offers. Our churches are often places known for their mediocrity and infighting, not as the source of a life-changing gospel.

For years now, I have sought to discern what gives some people the strength to go the distance and finish life well. I've prayed and kept a journal. I've watched and listened. I've interviewed and read.

I've discovered that it is not always the *skills* one has which determine success. Highly skilled doctors leave their practice every year. Great moms give up on difficult children. Many gifted teachers like Myra leave public schools every year. Promising young pastors like Rob leave the ministry after their first defeat.

It's not always the *opportunities* that determine success either. I've met people who had every opportunity—the right education, the right connections, the right breaks—but who fell apart at the first sign of difficulty. And many—in fact, most—of those I've talked to who have finished strong overcame tremendous obstacles to make it to the end of their lives with their faith, family, and character intact.

My observation, and the premise of this book, is that successful people have developed a comprehensive set of *attitudes and habits* that make all the difference. Right attitudes alone won't get you to the finish line unless you've also cultivated the habits of persistent people. And the right habits of persistent people won't get you there without the right frame of mind. It takes both.

Attitudes are when we learn to think correctly without acting.

Habits are when we learn to act correctly without thinking.

These habits and attitudes were identified first by looking at the common hurdles of life that frequently trip people. For instance, those who do not learn to deal with conflict find their lives becoming increasingly painful as unresolved issues throb within them. They become bitter, resentful old people, unable to enjoy life because of unresolved pain from the past. Learning to face up to conflict and invest in its resolution is essential if people are to avoid being tripped by the conflict hurdle.

I've identified twenty-one such hurdles. This list is no doubt incomplete; there are most likely other attitudinal and habitual hurdles that could be identified and overcome. But the ones you'll read about here are major stair steps toward that elusive state we call "success." You won't be equally impacted by each chapter. More than likely, you already have it together in several of these areas. But failure in just one of these can keep you from finishing well at life.

Dale Carnegie said, "Don't be afraid to give your best to what seemingly are small jobs. Every time you conquer one it makes you that much stronger. If you do the little jobs well, the big ones tend to take care of themselves."

I want to live my life with maximum results and minimal regrets. Don't you? Join with me as we take a journey, learning from the wins and losses of others, examining biblical examples, and putting into practice the habits and attitudes that will make us winners in this life and victors for all eternity.

CHAPTER ONE

Winners Work on Purpose

As the time approached for him to be taken up to heaven,
Jesus resolutely set out for Jerusalem.
—Luke 9:51

KEN HATCH WALKED INTO HIS HOME OFFICE early one morning fully intending to complete a major report due the next day. As he checked his morning E-mail, he wasn't surprised to see the thirty work-related messages. He *was* surprised to find a note from an old high school buddy, inviting him to their twenty-fifth reunion coming up the next summer. He took time to reply, and what he intended to be a brief synopsis of the last twenty years turned into a minor autobiography.

As Ken pulled up his calendar on the monitor to record the reunion, he saw a blinking reminder that his parents' fiftieth wedding anniversary was fast approaching, so he had to make calls to the caterer and the church where their reception would be held.

He still hadn't bought them a gift, so he pointed his Web browser toward an online shopping mall and spent some time looking for . . . something, he wasn't sure what. He finally found a gift he liked, paying for it with his credit card. When he went to print out the verification of purchase, he realized his printer cartridge was empty. There was no replacement in the supply drawer.

He glanced at his watch, checked it against the clock on his computer, and shook his head at the time. He would need that new cartridge to print his report. He had to drop by his accountant's office today anyway to sign some papers, so he jumped in the car for a quick trip to the local office supply store.

While there, Ken picked up a few other things he needed and a few things he really didn't. A quick trip through the "drive-thru" and a burger in a sack was on the passenger's seat. He began eating the burger as he headed to the accountant's office. There he found a line. It seemed like quarterly earnings time had brought in every self-employed man and woman in town.

While Ken was driving home, the low-fuel light began blinking on his dashboard. He drove past the entrance to his subdivision, headed toward the nearest gas station. While pumping his gas, Ken noticed they were running a special that day on oil changes across the street. He was several thousand miles overdue for one, so he paid for his gasoline and narrowly missed causing a wreck getting across the busy four-lane road.

"Bad news," said the technician. "We're out of filters for your model car. But Rudy is running out to pick one up, and he'll be back in a couple of minutes."

Ken glanced at his watch, certain it was running fast. He shrugged. No use getting worked up over something he had no control over. He had his cell phone in his pocket, so he called home, got his phone messages, and began returning them. His eighth-grade son had called. He was sick at the middle school and couldn't get hold of Mom. No wonder. She had gone on a field trip with their daughter's third-grade class. Ken found the phone number and called the school, explaining that he'd be by just as soon as he got his car serviced.

Rudy finally got back with the filter. The car was ready, and Ken realized he had no more cash. Worse, he had left his credit card on the desk earlier when he ordered his parent's gift. After leaving his driver's license as a hostage, he was finally able to leave. He raced to the school and picked up his son, who was a pale shade of green. He got home just as his wife and daughter did. He grabbed his credit card and headed back to the oil change place. Finally headed home for good, his cell phone rang. How did tacos sound for dinner? Great. Then could he stop by the store and pick up some cheese and a head of lettuce before he came home?

Another glance at the watch. *Already five o'clock.* He'd have to pull an all-nighter to get that report done.

As Ken walked in the house with the groceries, his fifth-grader greeted him with her soccer ball in hand. "Angela called and wants to ride with us to practice." Ken groaned. He had forgotten it was Thursday, the night he practiced with his eight-to-ten-year-old girls' team. If they had to pick up Angela, that meant they had to leave right away.

"I'll have dinner waiting when you get home," his wife said as they rushed out the door.

Ken never made it to the dinner table. By the time he got through with practice, he was violently ill with the same bug that had hit his middle schooler. He went to bed too sick to even think about the report that never got finished.

Ever had a day like that? Maybe I should ask if today was one of those days. Seems like one thing leads to another, and before we know it, the work hours are gone and we haven't gotten around to the most important task on our to-do list.

What's worse is that many people spend much of their lives running from urgent task to urgent task, never getting around to doing that for which they were created.

In the Scriptures we read that Jesus sensed his life's purpose quite early. After his parents took him to Jerusalem to celebrate the Passover, they headed back home, assuming their twelve-year-old was in the large group of family and friends who took the trip together. When nightfall came and he couldn't be found around any of the campfires, Mary and Joseph headed back to the city. They finally found him in the temple, amazing the scholars with his understanding. After they told Jesus of their fears when they discovered he was left behind, he tried to explain why he had lost track of time: "And He said to them, 'Why did you seek Me? Did you not know that I must be about My Father's business?' But they did not understand the statement which He spoke to them" (Luke 2:49–50 NKJV).

Learning to work on purpose is an essential habit of everyone who wants to finish well in life. No matter what your occupation, distractions abound. Most of us can keep quite busy without ever getting around to that which we are paid to do. All the technological advances that were supposed to help us work "smarter" have become work themselves. For many, answering the phone, responding to E-mail, and trying to figure out why the computer doesn't respond as it should seem like a full-time job.

I grew up in a remote mountain region in western New Mexico. I may be one of the last of my generation to know the meaning of the word *chores*. We heated our home with wood, so my brothers and I had to find, cut, haul, and then split firewood, as well as keep the wood box filled. We almost always had animals to take care of. Our cow needed milking twice a day. Pigs, chickens, rabbits, and pets had to be fed and their pens cleaned. Fences needed mending. The garden needed weeding and watering. In season, vegetables were waiting to be picked.

Then we had the usual childhood chores of keeping our rooms clean, washing dishes, and doing homework. But these were all just chores, not our primary work. Back then my "job" was being a student, or if it were summer, working on a neighboring ranch. Chores had to be done every day, but they were not substitutes for going to school or going to work.

Though I currently (regrettably) live in suburbia, it has been helpful to me to remember the difference between chores and work. My primary life's purpose, my work, is to communicate God's truths through writing and speaking, especially to those who have yet to discover his truths.

Though I have no livestock and our home has central heating, I still have chores. Because I'm a husband, father, staff member of a church, basketball coach, and neighbor, I have more than enough other interests and obligations to occupy my days and nights. If I don't carefully regulate my time and keep my focus, I can go for days, weeks even, without working on purpose.

I can't spend all day every day working on purpose; no one can. But I can make sure that I give significant time on a regular basis to what I know is my reason for being on this planet.

Salesmen have to sell. That's their purpose. Inventors have to invent. That's their purpose. Teachers have to teach. That's their purpose. But in any work environment, the paperwork and the meetings and the other chores can easily distract.

I have a friend who is a nurse. She got into nursing because she felt called to serve people. Because she was so good at what she did, she was promoted to a management position. Though she appreciates the bigger paycheck and has enjoyed some of her new responsibilities, she is largely dissatisfied with her job. She would do well to reconsider her purpose and ask if her current position is allowing her to work on purpose.

Knowing and living out our purpose helps us avoid getting sidetracked. Or at the very least, when we get sidetracked, we know how to get back on the right track. Other demands on our time may come for a season, but the person who works on purpose never allows those things to overshadow her real work, even if she can't get it right away.

Knowing and living out our purpose helps us avoid making costly mistakes. Time is of greater value than money. I can never regain lost time. I cannot put my time to work gaining interest. Time is our most precious resource, and we must learn to treat it as such.

Knowing and living out our purpose allows us to say no to those good causes that are not our cause. I have a budget for my money. When someone calls asking for a donation to some charity, I can explain that I've already budgeted for all my contributions for the year. In the same way, when I'm asked to take on a project or a ministry or to help with this or that, I have the freedom to say no if my time budget has nothing left.

Barriers to Fulfilling God's Purpose with My Life

I struggled early in my ministry with direction. Jim Danielson, associate pastor of the church we were attending, helped me pinpoint the source of my struggle. "When you're only interested in one thing," he said, "it's pretty easy to decide what to do. But if you have multiple talents and interests, it can be pretty difficult."

Attention surplus disorder. For years I had noticed that my curiosity, which I had always considered an asset, had become a liability. Instead of maintaining my focus on the few things I knew were part of my calling, I kept dabbling in any number of things that interested me. I dabbled with the guitar. I dabbled in oil painting. I dabbled in golf. The more I dabbled, the less time I had to become proficient in speaking and writing. I don't want to be a dabbler. I want to be proficient.

Poor time management. The best thing about the future is that it comes only one day at a time. Learning to live on purpose begins with working on purpose *today.* Simple time management techniques such as making a to-do list, then prioritizing the day's work can go a long way toward making sure that the most important tasks get done each day. If those daily high-priority tasks are made with your life's purpose in mind, you are well on your way toward working on purpose.

Not realizing I have a choice. Certainly we all get hit with unexpected demands on us, and we have no choice but to respond. But all too often we get caught up in someone else's expectations for our life, and drift along, not realizing that we have the freedom to choose something different. We almost always have more choices than we think. Some are riskier than others. Some are costlier than others. But the person who wants to finish well in life is willing to make the harder choice. Every "yes" to my life's purpose requires a corresponding chorus of "no's" to the conflicting purposes of others.

Finding God's Purpose for My Life

"You will never find God asking persons to dream up what they can do for Him," says Henry Blackaby in his landmark study *Experiencing God.*[2] Yet many Christians who have a more-or-less defined life purpose have never specifically sought the Lord's direction for their life's purpose.

At a writer's conference a few years ago, I heard novelist Robin Jones Gunn say, "If you agree to say yes to God's purpose for your life, you'll never be bored again by Jesus Christ."

Here's a basic reminder for anyone who considers himself or herself to be a follower of Christ: *God has the right to interrupt my life.* When I accepted him as Lord, I gave him the right to use me any way he wants. My self-defined life's purpose is "as filthy rags" compared to his purpose for me. Which leads to the next question: How do I discern God's purpose for my life?

In a book about finding a purpose for your marriage, Kevin and Karen Miller tell the story of a couple named Booth:

> For the first ten years of their marriage, William Booth, especially, was in a quandary: What was God calling him to do?
>
> Then his wife, Catherine, a skillful Bible teacher, was invited to preach in London. While they were there, William took a late night walk through the slums of London's East End. Every fifth building was a pub. Most had steps at the counter so little children could climb up and order gin. That night he told Catherine, "I seemed to hear a voice sounding in my ears, 'Where can you go and find such heathen as these, and where is there so great a need for your labors?' Darling, I have found my destiny!"
>
> Later that year, 1865, the couple opened the "Christian Mission" in London's slums. Their life vision: to reach the 'down and outers' that other Christians ignored. That simple vision of two people grew into the Salvation Army, which now ministers through three million members in ninety-one countries."[3]

Finding your purpose is a matter of finding the clues God has revealed already in you and through you. Begin by taking:

A look back. What were the things you were interested in as a teenager? Many young people have ignored their intuitive purpose because a well-meaning elder convinced them they would make a better "living" in business or some other field.

A look around. Many believers have ignored God's best purpose for their lives because it conflicted with their expectations for a particular lifestyle. Relational attitudes and other issues help clarify purpose and direction in life.

A look within. God is always more concerned with our spiritual well-being, while we tend to focus on our physical well-being. Is the life purpose you are considering one that will facilitate your growth in Christlikeness? Or do your personal ambitions have the potential to be spiritual shackles?

A look ahead. When life is almost over for you, which memories will be most important to you? Better yet, imagine yourself on Judgment Day. What life's work will allow you to hear, "Well done, good and faithful servant"?

On September 1, 1999, after eight stellar seasons with the White Sox, Frank Thomas hit rock bottom. He'd lost the edge on the baseball diamond; his last two years were mediocre. The Chicago sports writers were pounding him, and many were writing him off.

Thomas knew he had to do something, so he called his former hitting instructor, Walt Hriniak, for help. The front office agreed to bring Hriniak back in to try to salvage Thomas's career. After studying tapes of Thomas at bat, Hriniak discovered a mechanical problem with Thomas's swing. He'd lost the pace to the swing. It was too long and the movement of his head was jerky rather than smooth. Hriniak could fix those problems in less than an hour in the batting cage. But something else was wrong—something only Thomas could fix.

Thomas had lost his focus. Along with some family problems, he was getting hammered in the business world. "Big Hurt Enterprises," his sports marketing company, went belly up. His record company, "Un-D-Nyable," was draining his personal finances. Thomas had a decision to make: Would he continue to dabble in this and that, including his baseball career, or would he funnel his attention back into what made him great in the first place—baseball?

He made his decision. He put the distractions behind him and had one of the best seasons of his career. In baseball, as in life, focus is essential.

We will never get another chance at today. If we don't make intentional choices, based on our understanding of God's plan for our lives, we will be consumed by the purposes of other people. It's time to focus. We can't afford to wait until tomorrow. Set your course today and stick to it.

CHAPTER TWO

Winners Plan Tomorrow Today

"For I know the plans I have for you," declares the LORD,
*"plans to prosper you and not to harm you, plans to give
you hope and a future."*
—Jeremiah 29:11

I GLANCED AT THE CLOCK as the phone rang. 5:45 P.M.

"How soon will you be home?" my eleven-year-old daughter asked.

"Give me another thirty minutes here," I said. "I need to get ready for tomorrow."

"Why do you have to get ready for tomorrow tonight?" I gave her a quick answer and made a note to talk with her later that evening about the benefits and advantages of planning tomorrow today.

Is It Wrong to Plan?

Some people have cited Jesus' teaching in Luke 12:16–21 as proof that God does not want us to plan for the future. Is that what he meant?

> And he told them this parable: "The ground of a
> certain rich man produced a good crop. He thought to
> himself, 'What shall I do? I have no place to store my
> crops.' Then he said, 'This is what I'll do. I will tear
> down my barns and build bigger ones, and there I will
> store all my grain and my goods. And I'll say to myself,

"You have plenty of good things laid up for many years. Take life easy; eat, drink and be merry.'"

"But God said to him, 'You fool! This very night your life will be demanded from you. Then who will get what you have prepared for yourself?'

"This is how it will be with anyone who stores up things for himself but is not rich toward God" (Luke 12:16–21).

Did Jesus imply that God punished the man for making plans to expand his business? Careful examination of this passage makes it clear this is not the case. Verse 21 explains why God called him a fool. He was hoarding his treasure for himself, and he had no room for God in his plans. Look at how many times the words *I, my,* and *mine* show up in this passage. These words reveal much about this man's heart.

Planning is not a sin. In fact, I'd go so far as to say that *not* planning is a sin, because lack of planning will always lead to a waste of precious time.

Planning by the Book

The Bible really does have much to say about the value of planning wisely. Here are just a few verses that make it clear that God wants us to be wise stewards of every hour he has given us.

To man belong the plans of the heart, but from the LORD comes the reply of the tongue. All a man's ways seem innocent to him, but motives are weighed by the LORD. Commit to the LORD whatever you do, and your plans will succeed. The LORD works out everything for his own ends—even the wicked for a day of disaster. The LORD detests all the proud of heart. Be sure of this: They will not go unpunished (Prov. 16:1–5).

May he give you the desire of your heart and make all your plans succeed. We will shout for joy when you are victorious and will lift up our banners in the name of our God. May the LORD grant all your requests (Ps. 20:4–5).

The plans of the righteous are just, but the advice of the wicked is deceitful (Prov. 12:5).

Plans fail for lack of counsel, but with many advisers they succeed (Prov. 15:22).

If we would take such verses to heart, planning our days carefully would become second nature.

Planning Ahead

Before going into ministry, I worked as a sales representative for a large financial services company. My manager was Bob Mulleedy, a real professional in every sense of the word. Bob had the amazing ability to always appear unrushed and unruffled, yet he carried a heavy workload. This was my first job that required multitasking and strategic planning, and I was struggling. I had to find time for three primary things—finding prospective customers, making actual sales calls, then taking care of various administrative chores. These "big three" had to be fitted around meetings, phone calls, and interaction with others in my office.

I was good at the actual sales part, and I "closed the deal" a high percentage of the time because I could help people envision the benefits of strategic financial planning. I dreaded the prospecting and would put it off as long as possible. My dread for prospecting was nothing compared to my absolute hatred for administrative work. I had a bad reputation with our office manager for always being late with weekly reports and follow-up communication on recent sales.

I went to Bob with my struggles. I communicated my likes and dislikes honestly, and we sat together one evening as he taught me his daily routine. Bob taught me that planning was an investment and should never be seen as a waste of time.

Planning well allowed him to concentrate first on those tasks that would move him toward his goals in the most effective way possible, without being distracted by urgent but unimportant activities.

His system wasn't complicated, but it was consistent. Before leaving the office every evening, Bob took a few minutes to plan the next day's work. Over the years I've adapted Bob's planning process to fit my own life. Feel free to adapt it to yours.

Pray First

As I look ahead to the next day, I realize that I cannot possibly do everything expected of me by others. I cannot do everything on my to-do list. I cannot even do everything I *want* to do. So I begin with the only thing that makes sense—I offer my time once again to God. I believe in and teach a philosophy of stewardship that goes beyond putting money in the offering plate. Romans 12:1 says, "Therefore, I urge you, brothers, in view of God's mercy, to offer your bodies as living sacrifices, holy and pleasing to God—this is your spiritual act of worship."

My time is my only commodity—giving God my time *is* giving God my life. While God never forgets that truth, I do—easily. So I have to make a daily declaration that my life is not my own. Simple though this may sound, a great deal of the demands I feel lose their power over me when I remember who gave me this life and the reasons for which I have been called to serve him. I live by the belief that God will help me accomplish every task for which he created me. So I try to get those tasks clearly in focus.

Getting the Big Picture Second

I start making lists on a legal pad, using three categories to help me prioritize the work in front of me.

Kingdom priorities. When I realize that even those things I think of as significant will not be remembered a hundred years from now, it helps me evaluate my work in relation to eternity. Kingdom activities include sharing my faith in Christ, investing in other people's spiritual growth, and growing in my own relationship with God.

Why list these things first on my to-do list? Jesus said, "But seek first [God's] kingdom and his righteousness, and all these things will be given to you as well. Therefore do not worry about tomorrow, for tomorrow will worry about itself. Each day has enough trouble of its own" (Matt. 6:33–34).

Long-term priorities. There are things I want to accomplish over time that require I do some things immediately. Financial security in my later years requires that I invest some money now. If I want to meet a book deadline next year, I have to write five hundred words each day. If I want the conference I'm planning for next spring to come off without a hitch, I'd better make some strategic phone calls this week.

Those things that are still off in the future are easy to ignore. That's why I love the advice given to me by my former manager, Kevin A. Miller at Christianity Today, Inc.: "The sooner you get behind, the longer you have to catch up." If I perceive that I'm getting behind on that project that isn't due until next fall, it gives me a sense of urgency and a willingness to take some steps to catch up.

These first two categories could be deemed "important." Important tasks are those that will ultimately lead me closer to my life's purposes and achieve the goals I have set for myself.

Short-term priorities. Not every deadline is in the distant future. Sooner or later the future sneaks up on us. There will always be some things that simply have to be done tomorrow. These activities feel "urgent." There will be meetings I can't escape, appointments to keep, and work that must be done immediately to keep someone else's schedule on track.

Many writers on the subject of time management have noted that the day before leaving on a vacation is often the most productive day of work for many people. Why is that? Because on those days, we attack our short-term priorities aggressively, getting them done so we can leave without them hanging over our heads.

Everything else. No doubt this is the biggest category for many of us. Is there anything left in this category that really belongs in one of the others I've just listed? If so, I move it. If not, then the "everything else" pile will have to wait. And isn't it amazing how many times the things that sit in our "everything else" pile eventually don't need doing at all?

Using these categories helps me prioritize my work. It tells me what I must say yes to. And as we've already discussed, saying yes to one thing means saying no to something else. Another way of looking at prioritizing work is to ask, "What am I willing to give up today so I may have what I want tomorrow?"

Eat the Elephant One Bite at a Time

Like you, I have certain tasks that must be done weekly. Then I have big goals that will be reached over a long period of time. I try to remember that I can best control activity, not outcome. So I try to decide what activities must be done this week that will lead to my goal tomorrow. I break those weekly goals into daily goals.

For example, I start preparing next Sunday's sermon on Monday. All I may do is read the text carefully, pray about it, and scribble notes to myself. But by starting on Monday, I know in my head where I'm going, and I can be thinking about it at other times throughout the day. On Tuesday, I'll look at the commentaries and lexicons. On Wednesday, I'll get some sense of structure for the message and look for illustrations. By Thursday I can usually be committed to an outline so a handout can be printed for our congregation to follow along on Sunday and our technical director can develop a PowerPoint presentation. Then on Friday (OK, sometimes on Saturday) I finish the details. (I've had the experience of starting a sermon on Saturday, and trust me, that process never produces anything anyone would want to listen to.)

Your job has similar tasks that can be broken down. Identifying sequential steps to a bigger job is a vital skill for those who want to finish well.

Work in Blocks of Time

Years ago it dawned on me that in addition to prioritizing my work, I had to determine how much time to give to it. Another time management cliché is that "work will expand to fill all the time allotted." I've found that carving a workday into blocks helps me see how much uncommitted time I have and allows me to keep nonpriority chores from consuming my day.

For example, most mornings I spend a two-hour block of time studying for the next sermon or a Bible study. That isn't all the time I give to study, but it helps me start the day with something of kingdom importance.

I schedule two thirty-minute blocks—one in the morning, another in the late afternoon—to check E-mail and return phone calls. If I only give myself thirty minutes, I'll not waste time with chitchat or reading every E-mail chain letter that finds its way into my box.

I schedule a lot of lunch meetings, so I count the drive time and meeting time as a block. I have several predictable weekly meetings, and I try to keep a thirty-minute block free right after each meeting so I can immediately follow up on whatever work I received from attending that meeting.

By assigning specific tasks to specific time slots, I in effect set appointments with each of those tasks. I rarely if ever miss appointments if I've agreed ahead of time to be there.

Plan to Create More Time for Yourself

When I look ahead toward a busy day tomorrow, I sometimes feel the urge to jettison some personal activities I would enjoy doing so I can attend to both the urgent and important that I have lined up for the next day. I've gone that route and have often experienced the dullness of life that results from neglecting rest and recreation. Years ago someone passed along this anonymous poem:

If you put your nose to the grindstone rough
And keep it down there long enough,
You will soon conclude that there are no such things
As a brook that babbles or a bird that sings.
These three things will your world compose:
Just you, the stone,
And your ground-down nose.

I must make time for myself.

Someone else may control your calendar to a large degree. Often the things that are of greatest importance to us are not even on our boss's agenda. When that happens, we have to create time for ourselves away from the demands of others. There are two easy ways to do that.

First, cut your television viewing back to just a few hours on weeknights. Many Christians complain about a lack of quality programming available yet still spend two or three hours a day parked in front of the set. Cutting back to just those programs you really enjoy buys you time for more important things. Better yet, learn to program your VCR so you can watch your favorite programs at your convenience.

Second, get up earlier. If you get up one hour early each day for a year, you have effectively created almost ten additional working weeks.

So you aren't a morning person. Get over it. I know too many former night owls who now enjoy the benefits of getting up early. The body can be disciplined and trained to get up at whatever time you tell it to. If you moved from California to Georgia, your biological clock would be out of whack for a few weeks, but you'd soon adjust.

That is, in effect, all we do when we decide to get up earlier. What does that have to do with planning tomorrow today? We plan for getting up earlier by being motivated to go to bed earlier. I've found that going to bed earlier is never a problem if the television never comes on.

These two simple changes will buy you hours each day to read, write, pursue that hobby, or take that class you need.

I'm still trying to convince my sixth-grader of the benefits of planning tomorrow today. We're making progress. She carries a planner in her school backpack. She's learning to take better notes in class and write down her assignments. When she gets home, she is beginning to prioritize her homework, estimate how much time it will take, then decide if she wants to play first or get started on her homework immediately so she can do something fun later in the evening.

She has learned the hard way that putting off big projects until the night before they are due leads to many tears as well as shoddy work.

Planning tomorrow today lets me rest easy at night, knowing the stage is set to make the next day productive and rewarding. Planning my work and working my plan are essential components of finishing the race God has set before me.

CHAPTER THREE

Winners Know Character-Building Never Ends

But the LORD said to Samuel, "Do not consider his appearance or his height, for I have rejected him. The LORD does not look at the things man looks at. Man looks at the outward appearance, but the LORD looks at the heart."
—1 Samuel 16:7

CHARACTER HAS BECOME A RELATIVE TERM in our society. Public opinion surveys have pointed out in recent years that most people in our country no longer hold character high on the list of qualifications for public office. While politicians still frequently cite their sterling character as a reason to vote for them, when some sordid incident from the past highlights a character flaw, they respond predictably. "Some mistakes were made (they never mention who made the mistakes). Nobody's perfect." Is character overrated? Are there such things as "minor" flaws that really don't affect our effectiveness in accomplishing our life's purpose?

When the magnificent nine-hundred-foot cruise ship *Titanic* sank in 1912 on its first voyage from England to New York, fifteen hundred people died in the worst maritime disaster up to that time.

For years investigators held that when the *Titanic* hit an iceberg, it opened a huge gash in the side of the liner. But an international team of divers and scientists recently used sound waves to probe through the wreckage. Their discovery? The damage was surprisingly small. Instead of a huge gash, they found six relatively narrow slits. But those slits extended across all six of the watertight holds.[4]

The damage was small, below the water line, and invisible to most observers. But it sank a huge ship and brought grief and loss to thousands of families. In the same way small compromises, unseen to others, can ultimately sink a person's character.

Character, like the muscles of our bodies, dwindles quickly if not exercised frequently. Consider Walter, a successful accountant and a family man of deep personal convictions. In college, he submersed himself in the spiritual disciplines he learned while deeply involved in a campus ministry known for discipleship. He carried those disciplines into his marriage. For several years he memorized Scripture, fasted, exercised his spiritual gifts in service to his church, and was an enthusiastic student of the Bible. Walter made prayer a high priority in life. In large part due to his character, he received numerous opportunities for advancement in his career. Within a few years he became a partner in a significant firm and took on strategic leadership responsibilities.

As Walter grew older, the complications of a growing family and a pressure-cooker career began to steal time from his devotion to Christ. Though he maintained his moral convictions of right and wrong, his behavior gradually became inconsistent with his belief system. This created inner turmoil, which began to poison his relationships with others. His family sensed a growing distance in the way he related to them. His wife of thirty-four years, who had never had reason to distrust him before, secretly wondered if he was having an affair.

Walter's employees noticed a steady escalation of his use of inappropriate anger when dealing with staff conflicts. He went through three secretaries in a year as he became increasingly difficult to work with.

Walter had given up all his responsibilities at church because of his work schedule, but he remained faithful in attendance. But now he found more and more excuses to stay away on Sundays.

Finally, his adult son, Ron, dared to confront his father. After a long, painful meeting filled with denial and resentment, Walter ultimately admitted to a years-long addiction to Internet pornography. The shame and embarrassment of his confession almost destroyed him. He withdrew even further from his family, eventually separating from his wife and children. Though the issue remained a private matter in the family, it had devastating consequences for his career.

Walter's partners cared for him personally, but they had a company to run and couldn't wait for his recovery. Though it was called an "early retirement," everyone knew Walter was squeezed out.

Friends and colleagues would have once described Walter as a man of godly character. But they now knew his character was flawed. His careless treatment of sinful material had planted seeds of pain in every area of his life. Those seeds had taken deep root.

If a person's character takes a direct hit, is there hope for restoration? Could a person like Walter regain the integrity he had once known? Is character like virginity—once it's gone, totally gone and irretrievable?

A character study of a father and son from the Old Testament gives us the answer. David is one of the most complex men in all of Scripture. People recognized that David even as a young man had impeccable moral character. When Samuel the prophet came to Jesse's house, he immediately assumed the eldest brother, Eliab, was the logical candidate to be anointed as the next king of Israel. But the Lord had different criteria. "Do not consider his appearance or his height, for I have rejected him. The LORD does not look at the things man looks at. Man looks at the outward appearance, but the LORD looks at the heart" (1 Sam. 16:7).

We know David to be a man of great courage. Even as a teenager, he was willing to face Goliath, the champion of the Philistines, in mortal combat for blaspheming God and God's people.

David was willing to wait on the Lord's timing. Although Saul made numerous attempts on David's life, David refused on two different occasions to kill him and take the throne that had been promised to him (1 Sam. 24; 26).

He was gifted with great leadership ability. The nation of Israel expanded its borders and found unprecedented military advantage during his rule. David "reigned over all Israel, doing what was just and right for all his people" (2 Sam. 8:15).

David was compassionate, taking on responsibility for Mephibosheth, the crippled son of his friend Jonathan (2 Sam. 9), even though it was a politically incorrect move.

David was known throughout the nation as a man who was passionate about God. He demonstrated that passion through exuberant worship in public gatherings. "David, wearing a linen ephod, danced before the LORD with all his might, while he and the entire house of Israel brought up the ark of the LORD with shouts and the sound of trumpets" (2 Sam. 6:14–15).

First Samuel 30:6 reveals a key insight about this man. Where did he find the physical strength necessary for war, the emotional strength as well as the strength of character indispensable for leadership? "But David found strength in the LORD his God" (v. 6).

Yet even a man of David's spiritual maturity wasn't immune to a breach of character. For reasons we can only guess, one spring David decided to stay behind in Jerusalem when his army went off to war (2 Sam. 11). One night, unable to sleep, he went up to his rooftop porch and walked around, looking down over the city God had given him. Most houses were dark, their lamps long extinguished. But in one small home a light still burned. As David watched that tiny window, wondering who else was up that late, he caught a glimpse of a beautiful woman, naked from her bath.

That brief glance from a distant rooftop planted a seed of lust in David's heart. That seed took root and began to grow as he replayed it in his mind. He had to know who she was. His servant reported back that she was the young bride of one of his soldiers who was off fighting the Ammonites while his commander-in-chief stayed home. Unable to shake the mental image of her naked beauty, David had the young woman brought to his palace. Abusing the power and position God had given him, David impregnated her.

Anxious to cover his sin, David tried to get her husband home to sleep with his wife. When the young soldier displayed more character than his king, David sent word to put him in the thick of battle where he would be killed. David then made Bathsheba one of his many wives.

The prophet Nathan, the very man who had anointed David king many years earlier, was chosen by God to confront David about his sin. To David's credit he admitted his sin. Psalms 32 and 51 give us a record of his repentance and restoration.

In his later years, David appointed his son Solomon to succeed him on the throne and gave him instructions on how to be a man of character. First Kings 2:1–4 says:

> When the time drew near for David to die, he gave a charge to Solomon his son. "I am about to go the way of all the earth," he said. "So be strong, show yourself a man, and observe what the LORD your God requires: Walk in his ways, and keep his decrees and commands, his laws and requirements, as written in the Law of Moses, so that you may prosper in all you do and wherever you go, and that the LORD may keep his promise to me: 'If your descendants watch how they live, and if they walk faithfully before me with all their heart and soul, you will never fail to have a man on the throne of Israel.'"

Solomon got off to a good start as a character-driven leader (1 Kings 3). At Gibeon he offered burnt offerings. God appeared to him in a dream and told Solomon, "Ask for whatever you want." Solomon asked for wisdom, to be able to govern with discernment and fairness. God was so pleased with this request that he granted it, while also giving Solomon great prosperity and power.

Yet Solomon eventually had his crisis of character. Though God had repeatedly warned his people of the spiritual hazards of marrying those who did not worship the true God, Solomon took wives from neighboring countries. Although these marriages were primarily for political alliances, Solomon had his father's weakness for beautiful women.

First Kings 11:3–6 records these tragic words: "He had seven hundred wives of royal birth and three hundred concubines, and his wives led him astray. As Solomon grew old, his wives turned his heart after other gods, and his heart was not fully devoted to the LORD his God, as the heart of David his father had been. He followed Ashtoreth the goddess of the Sidonians, and Molech the detestable god of the Ammonites. So Solomon did evil in the eyes of the LORD; he did not follow the LORD completely, as David his father had done."

Sadly, the Bible contains no record that Solomon repented. It appears that after a long period of character-driven leadership, he finished his life far short of the will of God.

David tripped over a hurdle, but he got back up and finished the race. When Solomon stumbled, he dropped out of the race. Again, gaining and maintaining character is much like physical fitness. Even a world-class runner will lose her strength and endurance if she stays on the couch instead of going to the track. In issues of character, we really do "use it or lose it."

Although Walter the accountant floundered for almost a year, eventually he began the determined effort to rebuild the character he had lost. Although his sin did not become public, it did hurt a number of people, especially those who knew and loved him best. He has made every attempt to repair the damage he inflicted on them.

Walter's work with a counselor helped him determine the emotional root that led to his vulnerability to his particular sin, which has set him free. He has started his own business, and his career is doing even better than before. He has made himself accountable to a small group of men for his time, and he allows them to question his use of time so there are no opportunities for secret sins. He rebuilt trust with his wife and son over time by consistently demonstrating evidence of his repentance. Most of all, he's reinstated the disciplines of spiritual growth that keep him close to God and sensitive to God's Spirit.

Walter is well on his way toward finishing life in such a way that his children and their children will remember him with respect and admiration. He knows that a lapse of character is always possible, and he admits that the fear of falling again is a powerful motivator to keep clear of danger.

In his autobiography *I Almost Missed the Sunset*, Bill Gaither writes:

> Gloria and I had been married a couple of years. We were teaching school in Alexandria, Indiana, where I had grown up, and we wanted a piece of land where we could build a house. I noticed a parcel south of town where cattle grazed, and I learned that it belonged to a ninety-two-year-old retired banker named Mr. Yule. He owned a lot of land in the area, and word was that he would sell none of it. He gave the same speech to everyone who inquired, "I promised the farmers they could use it for their cattle."
>
> Gloria and I visited him at the bank . . . Although he was retired, he spent a couple of hours each morning at his office. He looked at us over the top of his bifocals.
>
> I introduced myself and my family and told him we were interested in a piece of his land. "Not selling," he said pleasantly. "Promised it to a farmer for grazing."
>
> "I know, but we teach school here and thought maybe you'd be interested in selling it to someone planning to settle in the area."

He pursed his lips and stared at me. "What'd you say your name was?"

"Gaither. Bill Gaither."

"Hmmm. Any relation to Grover Gaither?"

"Yes sir. He was my granddad."

Mr. Yule put down his paper and removed his glasses. "Interesting. Grover Gaither was the best worker I ever had on my farm. Full day's work for a day's pay. So honest. What'd you say you wanted?"

I told him again.

"Let me do some thinking on it, then come back and see me."

I came back within the week, and Mr. Yule told me he had had the property appraised. I held my breath. "How does thirty-eight hundred sound? Would that be OK?"

If that was per acre, I would have to come up with nearly sixty thousand.

"Thirty-eight hundred" I repeated.

"Yup. Fifteen acres for thirty-eight hundred."

I knew it had to be worth at least three times that. I readily accepted.

Nearly three decades later, my son and I strolled that beautiful, lush property that had once been pastureland. "Benjy," I said, "you've had this wonderful place to grow up through nothing that you've done, but because of the good name of a great-granddad you never met."[5]

Ironically, it was Solomon who wrote: "A good name is more desirable than great riches; to be esteemed is better than silver or gold" (Prov. 22:1).

A good name—a reputation as a man or woman of character—is a powerful legacy to leave our children. Keep working on it.

CHAPTER FOUR

Winners Focus Forward, Not Backward

Brothers, I do not consider myself yet to have taken hold of it. But one thing I do: Forgetting what is behind and straining toward what is ahead, I press on toward the goal to win the prize for which God has called me heavenward in Christ Jesus. All of us who are mature should take such a view of things.
—Philippians 3:13–15a

IN MY QUEST TO DISCOVER HABITS AND ATTITUDES that make a difference, I've developed a habit of asking pointed questions of people over the age of sixty. I tell them about the book I'm working on and then begin to ask what they've learned about living a purposeful life. Not everyone I've met feels they have lived such a life. In fact, before we've gone very deep in the conversation, some begin to express deep regrets over events long past.

One man told me, "You can never accomplish anything great if you neglect your family. If you fail at marriage, you have failed at life." He did not disclose all the details, but he went on to reveal that many years ago he had divorced his first wife, leaving her to raise their young son alone. He had later remarried and seemed to have a good relationship with his second wife and their now-grown children. But he was haunted by the failure of his first marriage, for which he took full responsibility. In fact, he began to berate himself in strong language that surprised me, considering that this failed marriage had happened almost forty years before.

Later I brooded over our conversation. When I had casually invited him to assess his life for clues about a life well lived, he immediately went to his great failure and refused to look beyond that event. I won't presume to read his mind, but it appeared to me that his failure controlled him so strongly that he was unable to enjoy life fully in the present. And it was certainly difficult to get him to look ahead to the future. It was as if he were driving through life looking in his rearview mirror.

This visit contrasted with another. Another man rose to the baited question and told me about his great accomplishments as an athlete. He had won a room full of awards and trophies. The more he talked, the more animated he became. Clearly, he considered himself a success because of his athletic achievement.

But he eventually revealed that he had not played his sport in more than thirty years. Furthermore, he had not invested what he had learned about the game in others. He had not coached, officiated, taken a role in the governing board of his sport—nothing. To use a football analogy, he was living his life in the fourth quarter, hoping that the points he scored in the first quarter would be enough.

He also appeared to be driving through life guided by the rearview mirror. That's how I came to the fifth habit of people who finish well: They are focused on an expectation of the future, not the failures *or* successes of the past.

Snapping Our Shackles

You can probably name some of your own friends and family who seem shackled to their past. The greater concern is whether you can recognize your own bondage.

Some become shackled by past hurts. None of us make it very far in life without being hurt by people we love. To be sure, some suffer more than others. And yet the degree of hurt is not usually what determines who moves on—and who gets stuck in the past.

Some become shackled to past failures and unfulfilled dreams. If we had perfectionists for parents, we may have been misinformed about mistakes. Some people feel they are near fatal—to be avoided at all costs. Some are indeed costly, but few mistakes involve permanent loss. Those who can't get over their past mistakes need to come to a new way of looking at them. Rather than seeing mistakes as something to be avoided, these mistakes need to be embraced as evidence that we are learning and growing. Creativity, for example, is a valuable quality, but one that cannot exist in an environment that won't allow mistakes.

Some become shackled to past successes. I'm convinced that too much success too early in life is more liability than asset. People who attain success too early tend to become prideful and lose sight of their need to depend on God. But those who have grown up with some success mixed with a healthy dose of failure are able to give God credit and to keep a humble spirit about them.

Some become shackled to past limitations. I heard another speaker once explain something I'd noticed at the zoo. Elephants have a habit of swaying back and forth on their front legs. This speaker said that a trainer had told him this behavior went back to an elephant's earliest days in captivity. A young elephant would be fitted with a heavy leather band around its foot, connected by a heavy chain to a deep stake in the ground. No matter how hard the young elephant pulled, he could not break free. Over time, his behavior changed to a habitual tug on the chain.

Once the elephant was fully grown, he possessed the strength to snap the chain if he chose to. But he was conditioned simply to sway back and forth, tugging gently on the chain.

This behavior is not just found in elephants; it's all too common among people. Too many of us are still listening to voices from the past that tell us, "You're stupid. You can't win. You're hopeless." We're much stronger now, thanks to Christ's dwelling within us. But we've conditioned ourselves to give little emotional tugs once in a while, believing those words are true. Some people live never knowing they could be set free from their past limitations and move to a preferable future if they only chose to do so.

Some become shackled to past sins. Guilt is a debilitating emotion. Legitimate guilt causes us to admit our sin, ask God for forgiveness, and turn away from sinful behavior. Illegitimate guilt is a favorite tool of the Evil One to keep Christians from experiencing the joyful life Christ has to offer us. To the person who says, "I just can't forgive myself," I reply, "Then you must have a higher standard than God does, because the Bible says 'he is faithful and just to forgive.'"

Looking Back Stunts Our Spiritual Growth

Looking to the past is a major cause of spiritual stagnation. Ask a group of people to tell about a time when God was especially active in their lives, and many will describe a time many years back, perhaps when they were in college or even high school. It's discouraging to realize that we are often banking on spiritual victories long past. The writer of Hebrews addressed this common tendency.

There is so much more we would like to say about this. But you don't seem to listen, so it's hard to make you understand. You have been Christians a long time now, and you ought to be teaching others. Instead, you need someone to teach you again the basic things a beginner must learn about the Scriptures. You are like babies who drink only milk and cannot eat solid food. And a person who is living on milk isn't very far along in the Christian life and doesn't know much about doing what is right. Solid food is for those who are mature, who have trained themselves to recognize the difference between right and wrong and then do what is right (Heb. 5:11–14 NLT).

Spiritual maturity is best understood as a journey, not a destination. As long as we draw breath, there is hope of a closer relationship with Christ. One of the best ways to envision this is to remember that one day we will finally know him fully. Only then will our walk be complete.

Do We Simply Ignore the Past?

I don't want to imply that we should ignore the past. That's where we've filed most of life's valuable lessons. We learn best from our mistakes. Having the ability to recall them is a valuable tool for navigating the future. We learn almost as much from our successes. Who would want to forget the joy of achieving something great? Likewise, the past gives us valuable clues regarding that which doesn't change—human nature. We can glean from past experience insights that will help us grow in our relationships with others. However, having access to the files of the past is different from having our future programmed by the past.

My life is a constant reminder that we serve the God of the second chance. Like many young adults, I made some poor choices that could have been disastrous. I had little understanding of how many vocational options life offered, and I had some early work experiences that were really tough. I could look back and yearn to have those wasted years back. Instead, I am grateful that I learned the value of hard work and have a breadth of experience to draw from that few people today can relate to.

I made a mistake in a romantic relationship. Thankfully, the girl I was engaged to broke the tie just a few weeks before the wedding. For several years, I was handicapped by that rejection. But God brought a healing that has given me his perspective on those days. What appeared to be a heartbreaking loss and total failure opened the door for a future I had never imagined possible.

I wouldn't want to forget where I've been. If I did, I couldn't fully appreciate the place where God has brought me.

How Do I Keep My Focus Forward?

It is never too late to let go of the past and embrace God's preferable future. But how?

Get some objective coaching from a third party. Like many Christian leaders, I've sometimes grown into patterns of thinking and behaving that limited my future-focus. At one point, I had to find a Christian counselor to help me pinpoint the source of chronic anger in my life. Had I not taken that step, I can easily see myself still seething from the events of those days. All of us can benefit from finding a friend, pastor, or spiritual advisor who can stand back with an impartial eye and tell it to us straight. Of course, this step presupposes a willingness to act on the counsel we receive.

Learn to dream again. I frequently find myself talking with people who have suddenly lost their job. While a few immediately land another job, most go through a period of grieving. In many cases, what they lost was more than a job. They lost a dream. Until their grief has run its course, they won't dream again. But when they come to the realization that every end is also a beginning, they can begin to unpack a new dream. It is interesting how often the new dream is really an old dream that got parked on a shelf somewhere along the way.

See yourself as an obstacle to overcome. Ralph Stayer, president of Johnsonville Foods, wrote "[This is the insight] I realized early and return to often. In most situations, I am the problem. My mentalities, my pictures, my expectations, form the biggest obstacles to my success."[6]

This is especially true when we allow bitterness and unforgiveness to keep us hobbled to those painful events of yesterday. The person who hurt me is not the problem. My unwillingness to forgive and move on is the problem.

Set higher goals. As I write this chapter, the 2000 summer Olympic games are being held. Last night, the women's 4 x 100 medley swim team just shattered the world record by over three seconds. This unbelievable achievement would never have happened if all four women had agreed, "Now remember, we can't swim any faster than the world record. That's as fast as anyone can swim."

Yet sometimes we set equally ridiculous limitations on ourselves by failing to set higher goals for ourselves in every area of life. When we expect more, we achieve more. I'll talk about goal-setting in greater detail in a later chapter. But here's another way of looking at the subject. Set goals in your:

- *Public Life*. This is how acquaintances perceive me to be. This is the easiest to manage because it only requires that I manage appearances.
- *Professional Life*. This is how my *colleagues* perceive me to be. Those who work closely with me know me better; therefore, change will have to be on more than just a surface level to impact my peers.
- *Personal Life*. This is how my *family* perceives me to be. Several studies have examined why pastors' children sometimes leave the faith. Every one of those studies concludes that, almost without exception, those who abandon their faith are those who saw inconsistency between their father's professional life and his personal life. When Daddy is one man in the pulpit and another at home, children conclude that Christianity is about hypocrisy. Who can blame them for failing to see a need for that same hypocrisy in their own lives?
- *Private Life*. This is how *God* knows me to be. It is impossible to fool God. Therefore, this is the level worthy of our best energy. When I allow God to set me free from my past, when I experience a new freedom in Christ, when I get a glimpse into his eternal plan for my life, personal growth is inevitable. I can no longer be bound to my past because my future becomes brighter than I dare imagine.

When God changes me at this level, every other level is affected. Those who know me best will have the most evidence. I no longer concern myself with public image, with managing appearances. I will treat acquaintances, peers, and family with a more genuine, unconditional love. I'll give others hope that the Christ-focused life gives us far more than eternal security; it gives us a hope for this world as well.

Find a focal point. Bear with me while I repeat myself. Finding God's best for my life is the key to fulfilling God's best for my life. Whatever the cost, however painful the process, seeking a clear sense of purpose is the best way to keep our past from holding us back.

One more Olympic illustration. Despite suffering three broken bones in her right foot six months before the Sydney games, Laura Wilkinson of the United States pulled off an upset in the women's platform final, taking the lead with her third dive and holding it through the final round to win the first U.S. gold medal in this event since 1964.

After Laura won the event, the announcer asked the predictable questions. "How do you manage the fear of leaping off a thirty-meter tower?"

"I just pick a spot and focus on it," Wilkinson replied.

Later in the interview the announcer asked, "Tell us how you managed to come from behind to win this event."

Laura's reply, "I can do all things through Christ who strengthens me." Focus. It's the only way to keep our goals clearer than our mistakes.

CHAPTER FIVE

Winners Have a Right Perspective on Work

I skate to where the puck is going to be, not to where it has been.
—Hockey legend Wayne Gretsky

WHY IS IT THAT IN A COUNTRY that offers so many ways to make a living, so many people are unhappy in their work? In an age of record low unemployment, why has the cartoon character Dilbert become the icon of the modern worker? Why do many women who work raising children and caring for the needs of a home feel remorse over not being in the paid workforce, while many who are in the eight-to-five grind feel guilty for doing so?

When I talk with those who have finished well, I've noticed they talk about their life's work in a totally different way than my peers do. The skeptics among us will say, "Of course, they had it a lot better in those days. There was job security back then, and it was easier to get ahead."

I don't believe that argument, knowing full well that many of our grandparents' generation worked in unsafe environments, without any kind of benefits and without many other perks today's workers take for granted. Nor will I generalize about an entire generation as having a better attitude toward work. I'm sure that many older adults hated their jobs as much as anyone working today. But there were and are some who look at work differently, and that different perspective makes all the difference.

Many of my generation and those who are younger have come to expect our jobs to be much more than a way to make a living. Work now needs to be fulfilling to our sense of self-worth, be an opportunity to develop personal skills on someone else's nickel, make a meaningful contribution to society—and deliver a large paycheck. In other words, we expect work to meet, if not all, at least the vast majority of our needs.

I don't believe the heroes who influenced this book had that same dependency on work. Some who have finished well ran their life's race in the marketplace, some in the church, some in government, and others in education. And then there were others who made their biggest impact *outside* their jobs. All of them were aware that work shapes us in powerful ways—some for good—and others in ways that cause physical, emotional, and spiritual harm.

Two Dangers

Allowing work to dominate our lives. As I talked with many people about finishing well over the past few years, so many didn't feel they had done so. The primary reason, especially for men, was regret over neglecting family in order to achieve success at work. This is a common concern, even among those who I believe are clearly finishing well. The price tag of success can be high, but its appeal can be so strong that we postpone other things—important things. These postponements are always temporary at first, with all good intentions to balance out priorities later. But those postponements become habits, and habits often take us places we never intended to go and leave us far longer than we intended to stay.

Jesus told the crowd on the mountain to "seek first his kingdom and his righteousness, and all these things will be given to you as well" (Matt. 6:33). How different would our lives be if we were so concerned about God's kingdom that it weighed on our minds with the same intensity that the burdens of work do? How differently we would make decisions and set priorities if we awakened with thoughts of devotion instead of thoughts of vocation?

Allowing work to influence our thinking about other areas of life. A win-at-any-cost philosophy may work well for a football coach, but it is potentially deadly to a marriage. Making financial decisions based solely on profitability may contribute to the bottom line, but this will keep a person from experiencing the joys of giving to a great need, even when it's costly. Corporate structure may be a necessity in a huge organization, but it can choke a small group Bible study to death.

Paul had a warning for us in Romans 12:2: "Do not conform any longer to the pattern of this world, but be transformed by the renewing of your mind. Then you will be able to test and approve what God's will is—his good, pleasing and perfect will."

Allow Your Work to Bring Glory to God

Many of us have developed the habit of compartmentalizing our lives, keeping work, home, and church in separate categories with different expectations and different rules in each category. How different this philosophy is from the biblical concept that teaches we are integrated beings with need of only one operating system—the transforming power of the indwelling Holy Spirit.

Although we may not at first identify with Paul's instructions to slaves in Colossians 3, they are just as relevant to today's workforce as they were in the first century. These are paradigm-shattering thoughts that will radically alter our perception about work and its relationship to matters of the kingdom.

Work can become an act of worship. Going to church and going to work are two very different acts for most people. But verse 22 suggests that the two actions needn't be all that different. "Slaves, obey your earthly masters in everything; and do it, not only when their eye is on you and to win their favor, but with *sincerity of heart and reverence for the Lord*" (Col. 3:22, emphasis added).

There are many passages that suggest that learning submission in any context has spiritual benefits (for example, Rom. 13:1–7; Eph. 5:21; Heb. 13:17; 1 Pet. 2:18). We gain those benefits when we grow in the awareness that, by our actions, we are either serving or rebelling; that whether the boss is watching or not, God is.

Work can become an act of service to God. If asked to list acts of service to God without having paid attention to this verse, how many of us would think of things we do in church—pray, sing praises, give our tithes and offerings, work in the preschool department—all acts of a more "spiritual" nature.

Verse 23 has the potential to change our work habits themselves. "Whatever you do, work at it with all your heart, as working for the Lord, not for men" (Col. 3:23). Regardless of how difficult our work environment may be, regardless of how irrational or cruel our boss might be, changing our *focus* on work can turn our job from an impossible situation into an act of service.

Work can provide us with eternal rewards. Perhaps there is no greater example of our tendency to compartmentalize than experiencing the tension of the previous sentence. Most of us have heard plenty of sermons warning us about the dangers of expecting eternal rewards from temporal things. Yet Paul writes, "Since you know that you will receive an inheritance from the Lord as a reward. It is the Lord Christ you are serving" (Col. 3:24).

Imagine the possibilities that open up when we learn to conceive of our work as having eternal consequences. By acting and reacting to the stress and strain of the work environment in a Christlike manner, we can actually make kingdom investments as we make a living.

Internal Attitudes

It's no secret that God often uses the most difficult situations in our lives to mold us into the image of his Son. As the pressure from the hands of the potter shapes the lump of clay on the wheel, God uses the pressures of work to shape our character.

Self-control. Ephesians 4:26–27 is a familiar verse: "'In your anger do not sin': Do not let the sun go down while you are still angry, and do not give the devil a foothold." We often think of this verse in the context of marriage, but that is only one place where it has relevance. How many people experience stress and anxiety in their jobs, then carry those anxieties home with them that evening, even go to bed with thoughts of work-related tension on their minds? If we allowed God to teach us, we could leave that anger behind and never lose another night's sleep in anger over our job.

Honesty. The workplace is a testing ground for another area of our character. Ephesians 4:28 warns, "He who has been stealing must steal no longer, but must work, doing something useful with his own hands, that he may have something to share with those in need."

Few Christians would actually steal money from the cash register or embezzle funds from the company account. But few of us are innocent of the sin of stealing time from our employer. Spending time each day with personal phone calls, running personal errands, long lunch breaks, personal Internet use, and other time wasters are areas of stealing that we need to admit to and repent from.

Moral strength. The workplace puts all kinds of temptations in front of us. We run the risk of developing relationships that could be inappropriate, even sinful. Our natural bent toward greed is fueled in a profits-first environment. We are faced with making profitable decisions at the expense of people, even of principle. For that reason, Ephesians 5:3 is of great relevance to our work: "But among you there must not be even a hint of sexual immorality, or of any kind of impurity, or of greed, because these are improper for God's holy people."

Dependability. This characteristic is in short supply in the marketplace today. More than one company has seen their best and brightest stars jump ship to work for the competition, taking with them valuable knowledge and market advantage. To a lesser but more common degree, notice the work habits in your office the next time the boss is out on vacation. Do people work with the same intensity when she's out that they do when she's in?

Ephesians 6:5–8 says, "Slaves, obey your earthly masters with respect and fear, and with sincerity of heart, just as you would obey Christ. Obey them not only to win their favor when their eye is on you, but like slaves of Christ, doing the will of God from your heart. Serve wholeheartedly, as if you were serving the Lord, not men, because you know that the Lord will reward everyone for whatever good he does, whether he is slave or free."

External Actions

Being a Christ-follower ought to make us better employees and employers. If we even attempted consciously to live up to the example of our Master, employers around the world would be wrestling with one another for the right to hire competent Christians first. Here are some ways to allow your work to point to Christ.

Work wholeheartedly. Think back to the best boss you ever had. You probably enjoyed working for him because he believed in you, trusted you, and expected good things from you. How did you respond to his trust? Most of us would make a list something like this: *I was self-motivated, industrious, prompt, and took the initiative.* Colossians 3:23 says, "Whatever you do, work at it with all your heart, as working for the Lord, not for men."

Watch your mouth. Is there any greater embarrassment in the world than making a crack about the boss to a bunch of coworkers, only to realize that she was within earshot? Our mouths can get us in trouble at work in a variety of ways. We need to think of our mouths as a natural disaster waiting to happen.

James 3:7–12 declares, "All kinds of animals, birds, reptiles and creatures of the sea are being tamed and have been tamed by man, but no man can tame the tongue. It is a restless evil, full of deadly poison. With the tongue we praise our Lord and Father, and with it we curse men, who have been made in God's likeness. Out of the same mouth come praise and cursing. My brothers, this should not be. Can both fresh water and salt water flow from the same spring? My brothers, can a fig tree bear olives, or a grapevine bear figs? Neither can a salt spring produce fresh water."

If we want to make a great impact on our work environment, we would do well to guard our words, for once released they can never be recalled.

Someone once told me I could choose to be a thermostat or a thermometer. A thermometer *records* the temperature around it. When we respond to difficulties the same way our peers do, we are being thermometers. On the other hand, a thermostat *controls* the temperature. As followers of Christ, we have the opportunity to set the standard in our environment. Here are two ways to do this.

• *Keep it positive.* Is there any environment where it is easier to develop a critical spirit than at work? Without even being aware of it, we can fall into patterns of criticism and complaining. But the Bible warns us, "Do not let any unwholesome talk come out of your mouths, but only what is helpful for building others up according to their needs, that it may benefit those who listen. And do not grieve the Holy Spirit of God, with whom you were sealed for the day of redemption" (Eph. 4:29–30).

• *Avoid gossip.* A while back, a colleague at church walked into my office with, "You'll never guess what I just heard about . . ." Without thinking, I grabbed the bait.

"What? Tell me," I asked, anticipating a juicy tidbit of information about a person who was giving us both a hard time. The information my peer shared confirmed our suspicions that our attacker was not nearly as spiritually mature as we were. We reveled in that revelation.

It wasn't until after he left that I realized I had just participated in an act that disgusts me—the passing and receiving of gossip. Proverbs 20:19 says, "A gossip betrays a confidence; so avoid a man who talks too much." Proverbs 26:20 advises, "Without wood a fire goes out; without gossip a quarrel dies down."

Had I been more in tune with the Holy Spirit within me, I could have chosen not to hear the supposed truth about that person. But by being a willing listener, I was just as guilty as the person who brought the information to my door.

I wonder what effect we could have on our work environments if we simply refused to participate in the gossip mill at work? Then, if we would quit "sharing" gossip with our Christian friends under the guise of "prayer request," we'd really make some headway.

Serve with a smile. "Every job has unpleasant duties, including this one. Deal with it. Learn to do them without grumbling, and you'll stand out from 95 percent of the people I've ever hired." This was the counsel given to me by a gruff manager early in my work life. He was right. This one bit of advice could revolutionize our impact on the workplace. That's why Paul's words in Philippians 2:14–15 are such good advice on how to make an impact on our workplace. "Do everything without complaining or arguing, so that you may become blameless and pure, children of God without fault in a crooked and depraved generation, in which you shine like stars in the universe."

Don't get defensive or angry when treated poorly. It would help us all if we would be prepared for unfair treatment in the world. It happens to everyone, believers and unbelievers alike. It's only a question of when. So how will we respond when treated unfairly?

"For it is commendable if a man bears up under the pain of unjust suffering because he is conscious of God. But how is it to your credit if you receive a beating for doing wrong and endure it? But if you suffer for doing good and you endure it, this is commendable before God" (1 Pet. 2:19–20).

Swallow our pride. How rare is it to see someone in the workplace apologize for hurting another? Rare enough to be the topic of conversation for days. We are so competitive and conscious of our place in the company pecking order that we have made a science out of blaming other people rather than taking credit for our own mistakes. Can you imagine how refreshing it would be for someone to apologize when they were wrong as a means of demonstrating a Christian core value? Again we go to Paul for advice: "Get rid of all bitterness, rage and anger, brawling and slander, along with every form of malice. Be kind and compassionate to one another, forgiving each other, just as in Christ God forgave you" (Eph. 4:31–32).

Look out for people. While everyone else is looking out for the bottom line, profits, quotas, sales reports, balance sheets, budgets, and keeping an eye on the competition, who is looking out for the well-being of you and your peers? One of the most significant ways we can make a difference in the climate of our workplace is to make people our first priority.

Regardless of your title or position, you can begin immediately to be the advocate for people around you. When people who are without Christ have a hurt, to whom can they go for comfort? Since they don't have a pastor or Christian friend, who will give them counsel?

God has placed you in the office, shop, school, or neighborhood where you work in order to be his presence there. You are called to be a missionary. How will you respond to that opportunity?

It will take a servant heart to be effective. Philippians 2:4–7 teaches, "Each of you should look not only to your own interests, but also to the interests of others. Your attitude should be the same as that of Christ Jesus: Who, being in very nature God, did not consider equality with God something to be grasped, but made himself nothing, taking the very nature of a servant, being made in human likeness."

Those who finish well know that their greatest impact may not be the sales they make, the contracts they write, the surgeries they perform, or the awards they win, but the lives they influence for Christ. When a job is just a job, our expectations aren't that high. But when our job becomes our ministry, we gain a whole new perspective.

CHAPTER SIX

Winners Bounce Back from Adversity

*Let us not become weary in doing good, for at the proper time
we will reap a harvest if we do not give up.*
—Galatians 6:9

BRUCE SHELLEY, senior professor of church history at Denver
Theological Seminary, is another hero of mine who is finishing
well. Dr. Shelley tells a parable about a farmer whose old dog
fell into a dry well. After assessing the situation, the farmer sym-
pathized with the dog but decided that neither the dog nor the
well was worth the trouble of saving. Instead he planned to bury
the old dog in the well and put him out of his misery.

When the farmer began shoveling, initially the old dog pan-
icked. But then it dawned on the mutt that every time a shovel
load of dirt landed on his back he could shake it off and step up.
This he did blow after blow. "Shake it off and step up, shake it
off and step up, shake it off and step up!" he repeated to encourage himself.

It wasn't long before the dog, battered and exhausted,
stepped triumphantly out of that well. What he thought would
bury him actually benefited him—all because of the way he han-
dled his adversity.

That story always reminds me of a biblical character who
more than once found himself about to be buried in some hole.
In Genesis 37 we find that Joseph was the favorite son of Jacob,
later called Israel. Because of his father's blatant favoritism and
Joseph's prideful attitude, his brothers despised him and took

advantage of an opportunity to get rid of him. At first, they abandoned him in a dry cistern to die. But his older brother, Judah, had second thoughts.

"Judah said to his brothers, 'What will we gain if we kill our brother and cover up his blood? Come, let's sell him to the Ishmaelites and not lay our hands on him; after all, he is our brother, our own flesh and blood.' His brothers agreed. So when the Midianite merchants came by, his brothers pulled Joseph up out of the cistern and sold him for twenty shekels of silver to the Ishmaelites, who took him to Egypt" (Gen. 37:26–28).

Once in Egypt, Joseph was sold to the captain of Pharaoh's guard, Potiphar. Because the Lord's favor was evident in him (Gen. 39:3), Joseph quickly became head of Potiphar's staff.

Unfortunately, his master's wife also took a liking to Joseph and tried to seduce him. When he refused her advances, she grew angry, and accused him of attempting to rape her. "Joseph's master took him and put him in prison, the place where the king's prisoners were confined" (Gen. 39:20).

But even imprisonment could not keep Joseph down. His trustworthiness and leadership skills gained the attention of the prison warden, who put Joseph in charge of all the prisoners. Two of Pharaoh's staff were also imprisoned there, and Joseph correctly interpreted some dreams for them. Upon his release, the king's cupbearer promised to intercede with Pharaoh on Joseph's behalf. But it didn't happen. "The chief cupbearer, however, did not remember Joseph; he forgot him" (Gen. 40:23).

Years went by before the cupbearer remembered his promise. Pharaoh had troubling dreams, and Joseph was called to interpret them. Through insight from God, Joseph did so correctly, warning that there would be seven seasons of plentiful crops, followed by seven years of drought and hardship. Joseph suggested setting aside 20 percent of the abundant harvest each year as insurance against the coming drought. Pharaoh was stunned by this young Hebrew's wisdom and insight.

"So Pharaoh said to Joseph, 'I hereby put you in charge of the whole land of Egypt.' Then Pharaoh took his signet ring from his finger and put it on Joseph's finger. He dressed him in robes of fine linen and put a gold chain around his neck. He had him ride in a chariot as his second-in-command, and men shouted before him, 'Make way!' Thus he put him in charge of the whole land of Egypt" (Gen. 41:41–43).

In the chapters that follow, Joseph was reunited with his family and was able to save them from the drought as well. Looking at this account from Scripture, I'm impressed by Joseph's resilience and ability to bounce back from disappointment and losses, even though most were not of his own doing.

What kept Joseph going? What was his secret?

Principles of a Resilient Person

A resilient person has a strong sense of being chosen. While still a boy, Joseph had a dream that he would lead his family in some way (Gen. 37:5–11). That sense of destiny must have sustained him throughout his long season of captivity. Joseph's response to his brothers when they are finally reunited gives evidence of that. "And now, do not be distressed and do not be angry with yourselves for selling me here, because it was to save lives that God sent me ahead of you. For two years now there has been famine in the land, and for the next five years there will not be plowing and reaping. But God sent me ahead of you to preserve for you a remnant on earth and to save your lives by a great deliverance" (Gen. 45:5–7).

Some may struggle with this, thinking, *I've never sensed God calling me to do anything.* But the Bible assures us that God chose those who would respond to his love to be his messengers, both across the street and around the world.

"But you are a chosen people, a royal priesthood, a holy nation, a people belonging to God, that you may declare the praises of him who called you out of darkness into his wonderful light. Once you were not a people, but now you are the people of God; once you had not received mercy, but now you have received mercy" (1 Pet. 2:9–10).

Because God has chosen you, he has invested in you, purchasing your freedom in Christ and equipping you to fulfill your purpose through the indwelling of his Spirit and the gifts of the Spirit.

A resilient person develops a problem-solving approach to life. The text gives few details about how Joseph gained the favor of both Potiphar and the prison warden, but his advice to Pharaoh paints a portrait of a man who knew how to solve problems. Historians find little precedent of any ancient government managing its resources in such a remarkable fashion. Joseph's solution came from the same source as the interpretation of Pharaoh's dream—God gave it to him.

To suggest that Egypt store a portion of the grain harvest during the seven years of abundance to be used in the lean years ahead shows a willingness on Joseph's part to think outside the box. Two examples from American history demonstrate similar creative thinking in action.

William Wrigley Jr., the Wrigley's gum founder, ran away from home at the age of eleven to escape working in the family's soap manufacturing business. He went to New York, where he sold newspapers, but soon was back home. In 1891 he left for good, going to Chicago to make his fortune. In the beginning Wrigley continued to sell soap, offering a free can of baking powder as an incentive to his buyers. Soap sales weren't that strong, but people loved the baking powder, so he started selling it exclusively while now offering two pieces of gum as an incentive. He soon discovered that the gum was even more popular than the baking powder, so Wrigley went into the gum business.[7]

The name Levi Strauss is synonymous with blue jeans in American culture. But the man by that name wasn't thinking about jeans when he went to California in hopes of making his fortune during the gold strike of the 1840s and 1850s. He did make a fortune, but not the way he had planned.

He set out with a load of heavy canvas fabric, from which he planned to sell sections for tents and wagon covers. Upon arrival, the first miner who saw his product said, "You should have brought pants." The seasoned miner further explained how there weren't any pants strong enough to endure the tough conditions of mining. Levi Strauss immediately made the miner a pair of work pants, and thus struck gold.[8]

When things don't turn out the way you are anticipating, don't panic. Don't dwell on what went wrong. Instead, focus on what to do next. Spend your energies on finding a solution so you don't repeat your mistakes. Consider the following questions when trying to determine the next course of action:

- Where can I get more information?
- Whom can I consult who has dealt with this before?
- How can I transform this disaster into an opportunity?
- What would my hero do?

A resilient person avoids infection from the victim mentality. Nowhere in this biblical narrative do we see Joseph feeling sorry for himself or blaming others. He simply took each situation as it came and made the best of it. The biggest problem in life is not having problems. Our problem is thinking that having problems is a problem.

Jesus warned us in John 16:33, "I have told you these things, so that *in me* you may have peace. In this world you will have trouble. But take heart! I have overcome the world" (emphasis added).

Every setback is an opportunity to grow in dependence on the Lord. Jesus contrasted two contexts, life in him and life in this world. One, he said, was peaceful. The other, troublesome.

I consider the following to be the most irritating verses in the Bible: "Consider it pure joy, my brothers, whenever you face trials of many kinds, because you know that the testing of your faith develops perseverance. Perseverance must finish its work so that you may be mature and complete, not lacking anything" (James 1:2–4).

Hebrews 12:7, 11 says, "Endure hardship as discipline; God is treating you as sons. For what son is not disciplined by his father? . . . No discipline seems pleasant at the time, but painful. Later on, however, it produces a harvest of righteousness and peace for those who have been trained by it."

I understand these verses. I believe them. I just don't like the implications. Problems are to life what weight-lifting is to exercise. Just as muscles are strengthened when they are taxed, so our character is strengthened when we face adversity.

Back in the early 1990s I pastored a church in Arizona. Just north of Tucson, outside the tiny town of Oracle, a giant greenhouse went up, covering over three acres. For two years, scientists sequestered themselves in this artificial environment called Biosphere 2. Inside their self-sustaining community, the Biospherians created a number of minienvironments, including a desert, rain forest, and savannah. Nearly every weather condition could be simulated except one—wind.

Over time, the effects of this windless environment became apparent. Within two years, a number of small trees bent over and even snapped. Without the stress of wind to strengthen the wood, the trunks grew weak and could not hold up their own weight.

When I read that account in the local paper, I found the metaphor I needed to sustain me through a particularly difficult period in ministry. The struggles I was facing in my church and in my own heart were the means by which God was strengthening my will and my character to be used by him for other things down the road.

Anticipate Change

At every turn of events, the Bible says that "Joseph prospered . . . the Lord gave him success . . . the Lord was with Joseph and gave him success in whatever he did." His success was due in part to his ability to anticipate change. In his first proposal to Pharaoh, Joseph told him they should store grain for the nation's own use. But after the famine began, the grain bins were so full and the famine was so widespread that Joseph soon discovered that the neighboring nations were suffering too. He began to sell them food as well.

The ability to anticipate and implement change is another skill that usually is rewarded in life. But not always. Seth Godin tells the following story:

> After my first year at Stanford Business School, I went to see Jim Levy, then-president of Activision, Inc., which, at the time, was arguably one of the fastest-growing companies in the history of the world. Activision made games for the Atari 2600 game system and was rolling in dough. I wanted to work for Levy for the summer.
>
> My bold proposal: "Hey, you've got all this cash and all these smart marketers and programmers. Why not go into the computer game business? You can dominate the PC the way you dominate the Atari 2600."
>
> "Looking back 25 years (yikes, that's a long time ago), that wasn't such a bold proposal. After all, the PC market was only an inch or two away from the market that Activision was already in. But Levy disagreed with my proposition and almost had me removed from his office by force. He told me, "We're in the cartridge business—and those machines use floppy disks. Forget it."[9]

Keep a kingdom perspective. There is evidence throughout these chapters that Joseph had a strong sense all along that God was in control. As his story concludes, Joseph reassured his brothers with these words: "You intended to harm me, but God intended it for good to accomplish what is now being done, the saving of many lives" (Gen. 50:20).

The ability to bounce back from adversity is easier if a person believes that God is in control, even when circumstances appear hopeless. The apostle Paul knew that, and he wrote these words about his arrest and imprisonment:

Now I want you to know, brothers, that what has happened to me has really served to advance the gospel. As a result, it has become clear throughout the whole palace guard and to everyone else that I am in chains for Christ. Because of my chains, most of the brothers in the Lord have been encouraged to speak the word of God more courageously and fearlessly.

It is true that some preach Christ out of envy and rivalry, but others out of goodwill. The latter do so in love, knowing that I am put here for the defense of the gospel. The former preach Christ out of selfish ambition, not sincerely, supposing that they can stir up trouble for me while I am in chains. But what does it matter? The important thing is that in every way, whether from false motives or true, Christ is preached. And because of this I rejoice (Phil. 1:12–18).

Some wise guy said, "Experience is what we get when we don't get what we were expecting to get." People who are resilient gain far more than experience from their disappointments. They discover new opportunities, new markets, new possibilities. Since the 1980s, hundreds of thousands of people have suddenly lost their jobs as corporate America has moved through cycles of binging and purging of people. Some of those people who once thought their lives were over will now look back to their downsizing as the pivotal point in their lives. It was in that point of despair that they found the freedom to make some new choices, to explore new opportunities, and to pursue some old dreams. This led them to the place of satisfaction they now enjoy.

As a father of two daughters, I'm quite familiar with the residents of the One Hundred Acre Woods, made famous in the *Winnie the Pooh* books by A. A. Milne.

My favorite character is Tigger, the loveable extroverted . . . well, tigger. Tigger bounces on his tail everywhere he goes. His mode of motion also describes his attitude. He never gets down for long; his nature is to bounce back from adversity. Tigger likes to sing a song about himself that says in part,

> The wonderful thing about Tiggers
> Is Tiggers are wonderful things.
> Their tops are made out of rubber,
> Their bottoms are made out of springs.

Maybe if we had tops of rubber and bottoms of springs, we would become more resilient. The focus of counseling was once on helping people feel good about themselves. The problem with that goal was that as soon as you reached it, another life event came along and washed away those temporary feelings. Now the goal of many therapists is to help people learn to overcome adversity. Resilience can be—and must be—learned if we are to grow beyond our difficulties.

CHAPTER SEVEN

Winners Evaluate Relentlessly

Therefore I do not run like a man running aimlessly; I do not fight like a man beating the air. No, I beat my body and make it my slave so that after I have preached to others, I myself will not be disqualified for the prize.
—1 Corinthians 9:26–27

PICTURE THE COCKPIT of a commercial airline. Knobs, gauges, levers, buttons, switches, and warning lights by the hundreds. What do they all mean? Not much to the passengers, but they mean everything to the pilot. The most important indicators are most prominently displayed in the pilot's field of vision. Throughout the flight, the pilot is continually evaluating altitude, fuel levels, oil pressure, speed, and a dozen other indicators of the condition of the aircraft and the flight. If any indicator deviates from what is normal or intended, he or she can immediately initiate corrective measures.

People who finish well have learned to evaluate different areas of their lives constantly, detecting little problems before they become big problems. Catching a potential error early could mean the difference between arriving safely at your preferred destination—or crashing.

Evaluate My Attitude

Excuses. When I was in the Air Force, my first sergeant was quick to interrupt anyone making excuses by saying, "I don't want to hear about the labor pains. Just show me the baby." When I find myself making a lot of excuses about things, that is a clue that I should stop and investigate my attitude. Excuses are evidence that I don't have a baby to show, or I'm ashamed of that baby. The reasons why will help me get back on track.

Shortcuts. Performance-enhancing drugs have become the curse of modern athletics. In just about every sport the desire for results can lead to an overwhelming desire to take short-cuts—shortcuts that can have devastating consequences. When I begin to look for ways to shortcut a Bible study I'm supposed to teach by plagiarizing someone else's outline, it's a hint that I'm unwilling to allow God's Word to percolate through my own being first. Not good for me or for those I would teach.

A critical spirit. Why else would I invest the emotional energy in criticizing someone or something else except that I have forgotten God's grace and longsuffering with me? Cynicism is sin. The sooner I deal with it, the better for me and everyone else around me. Becoming a grace-giver as well as a grace-receiver becomes my next priority.

Evaluate the Health of Relationships

A man came to see me some time ago. He was in agony because his marriage was falling apart. He had been vaguely aware of some stress in the relationship for a while, but the stress level had been tolerable. But after years of warning signs, his wife finally told him she was moving out. This caught him by surprise and prompted him to action.

In our initial conversation, he painted the portrait of a victim. Not only was his wife a pain to live with, but his last three jobs (in four years) had been torturous stints where he was tormented by despotic bosses. Not only that, but his parents had been mean and difficult people as well.

I had the difficult task of pointing out to him that if just about every relationship in his life was difficult, perhaps he was the more difficult party.

None of us want to believe we are the problem in relationships. So we fall into the blame game. While it feels good for a while to revel in the role of the victim, we'll never achieve our life's purpose that way. Mature believers have trained themselves to see trends in behavior that may be clues to a problem. Am I avoiding certain people? Lately, am I feeling hurt by people more than usual? Do I feel taken advantage of or taken for granted? Do imaginary angry conversations with people occupy my think time?

All of these can help me determine if I have allowed my attitude to drift. The solution comes when I determine the nature of my attitude. It will probably involve forgiveness and repentance for harboring bitterness and allowing self-pity to take up residence within me.

Evaluate My Adaptation to Change

God is in the people-changing business. This is a fundamental truth, yet many of us have an initial resistance to change of any kind. When we begin to grow in maturity and grace and experience the change it brings, the fear of change loses some of its bite. Paul understood that. Throughout his letters he intermingled instruction for personal change with instruction and admonition for corporate change in the church.

It helps when I consider that sanctification is a lifelong process of becoming like Jesus, and none of us really enjoy that painful process, even when we desire it deeply. It is then easier to understand why most change is so difficult and complex.

Evaluate My Commitment to My Goal

One of the most memorable moments in Olympic history came out of Mexico City in 1968. From the cold darkness came John Akhwari of Tanzania. Pain hobbled his every step. His leg was bandaged and bloodied, evidence of a terrible fall early in the race. The winner of the Olympic marathon had crossed the finish line over an hour earlier. Only a few spectators remained as the slight man hobbled toward the finish line. When he crossed that line, those left in the crowd roared their appreciation. Afterward, a reporter asked Akhwari why he had not pulled out of the race when it became apparent he had no chance of winning. He seemed confused by the question.

Finally he answered, "My country did not send me to Mexico to start the race. They sent me to finish the race."[10]

John Akhwari demonstrated a rare character quality that acknowledges that, in the long run, results are more important than effort. While he did not win the race, he did finish. No one could have faulted him for dropping out, given his injuries. Yet he chose to persevere and finish the race he had begun.

Evaluate the Execution of Strategies

Achieving success, that is, fulfilling your life's purpose, can be expressed like a mathematical formula: God-honoring Goal + Consistent Effort + Effective Strategy = Tangible Results.

God-honoring goal. Vision will only take you so far. Being able to see God's preferable future for your life does not ensure it will become reality. Hope is not a strategy. Wishing it to be so will not make it happen.

The strategy by which we attempt to fulfill our life's purpose is critical, yet this is often the factor we neglect most. Don't confuse activity with accomplishment. Hard work will only take you so far. It is possible to work at a grueling pace and not accomplish anything.

Consistent effort. In most areas of life, "trying hard" doesn't count for much. Millions of people say they are following an exercise program, yet they never see results in increased fitness. Millions more are seeking weight loss solutions through diets that don't produce lasting results. Churches around the world are engaged in evangelism strategies that result in few if any people coming to Christ. All would say, "But we're working hard at it." So what!

Effective strategy. What kind of strategy is worthwhile?
• One based on unchanging principles. Discovering those principles is the first step toward approaching any problem in life. Why is it that the Bible is so often our last resort, rather than our first?
• One that takes contingencies into account. There are too many variables in life to write a strategy in ink. Every athletic team, every army takes the field with a strategy in mind, based on principles. But if conditions are different than expected, wise coaches and military leaders can quickly modify or even scrap a strategy on the spot, adjusting to the reality around them. If your strategy has no flexibility, find another strategy.
• One that results in tangible measurements of success. Will you recognize success when you see it? Paul was able to look back upon his life and see visible evidence that he had accomplished his purpose. His legacy was the presence of churches around the Mediterranean perimeter. How will you know when you succeed?

We often comfort ourselves by saying, "At least we are faithful." I've often used "faithfulness" as an excuse for not rethinking my course of action. I'm not seeing results, but I will insist that working hard is enough. That's ridiculous. If we are consistently failing, it's time to reevaluate our strategy.

Evaluate My Core Competencies

One of my colleagues at church recently went through a season of life that left her stressed and anxious, especially about ministry. She struggled to find out why, since she had always enjoyed her work.

An occupational hazard of ministry is constantly being asked to serve others in areas outside of one's gifts. People will often assume a minister is equally competent at all types of ministry. My friend had done some marriage counseling for a couple, which prompted them to tell another couple. Before she knew it, she was swamped with counseling appointments. In spite of the success she found in helping couples reconnect, she felt increasingly drained.

A wise friend finally intervened and told her, "You need to go back to teaching spiritual gifts and plugging people into satisfying ministry. That's it. Say no to the counseling and say yes to what God has gifted you to do."

Within a few weeks, the joy she had once found in ministry returned. "I just lost sight of the main thing," she said.

Bright people are continually exploring and growing in new areas. While that growth is rewarding and stimulating to a point, it can coax us beyond the areas in which God has called us to serve. That's why all of us could benefit from asking, "Is most of my time being spent on things that fit my core competencies—the things I do best?"

The Bible teaches us, "Each one should use whatever gift he has received to serve others, faithfully administering God's grace in its various forms. If anyone speaks, he should do it as one speaking the very words of God. If anyone serves, he should do it with the strength God provides, so that in all things God may be praised through Jesus Christ. To him be the glory and the power for ever and ever. Amen" (1 Pet. 4:10–11).

Evaluate My Learning Deficits

"If the ax is dull and its edge unsharpened, more strength is needed but skill will bring success" (Eccles. 10:10).

In Solomon's example, there are two solutions—swing harder or sharpen the ax. This metaphor for personal development has been around for decades, but it still accurately conveys an image.

The question is not, "Will I continue learning?" Today it must be, "Where do I need to enhance my knowledge the most?"

Evaluate My Spiritual Vitality

I was flipping channels one night before bedtime and landed on *The Crocodile Hunter*, a staple of the Animal Planet channel. In each thirty-minute episode, Steve Erwin from Australia is capturing, chasing, and being chased by crocodiles, venomous snakes, and spiders—and anything else the producers can think of to elevate the adrenaline of the audience.

On this particular night, the host was attempting to capture "the world's most venomous snake." (Erwin catches snakes by grabbing their tails and spends several minutes playing with them before placing them in a bag. Part of the fun of watching is wondering when he's going to finally get his just reward for such behavior.)

I was really getting into this program, leaning intently toward the TV. As he made another reach for the snake's tail, it struck at him. At just that exact moment, a fly landed on my forearm. I shrieked and jerked so hard the remote control flew across the room. My wife, who was reading, screamed along with me for moral support. "What happened?" she asked.

"I don't know," I croaked, as I fell on the couch. While the Crocodile Hunter was bagging his snake, I was wondering if the fact that my left arm had gone numb was a sign I was having a heart attack, or if I had whacked it on something as I was attempting to dislodge the poisonous snake that hadn't bitten me.

After the adrenaline receded, we hooted over my reaction. Unable to keep a good story to myself, I shared it with our congregation the next morning during our call to worship. They laughed at (with?) me, but really tuned in when I made a spiritual application.

"Don't be surprised if the Holy Spirit touches you today. If you are not expecting his touch, you may not react in the way you want to. But if you came this morning expecting to hear from God and are open to receiving his word into your life, you'll recognize his touch and not be alarmed by it."

I'm not saying that we had a rerun of Pentecost that morning, but I think that people did engage the notion that God might actually reach out and touch them that morning. If it's been a while since I have sensed the touch of God's Spirit, something is out of whack.

Evaluate My Health Habits

Weight control is one of the perennial struggles of my life. It is also an accurate indicator of my emotional health. When I'm handling stress well, I can discipline my eating habits. When I begin to crave junk food and sweets, that's a good indicator of stress. Learning to monitor weight loss or gain, sleep patterns, dietary changes, and loss of interest in physical activities is an essential part of getting the most out of life.

In recent years, I have grown increasingly convicted about maintaining disciplines for good health. What poor stewardship it would be for me to die prematurely as a result of my own unrestrained appetites. Gluttony doesn't get a lot of press these days, but I'm convinced it is a symptom of a greater spiritual problem.

Do unto Yourself . . .

Learning to evaluate myself relentlessly can degenerate into a self-critical spirit that denies the reality of who I am in Christ. Paul's metaphor of beating his body should not be taken as a cue to abuse oneself, either physically or emotionally.

For years I struggled with appropriate self-evaluation. On one extreme, we can avoid evaluating our progress for fear of what we'll discover. On the other, we can become so self-critical that we discourage ourselves. My problem? I treated myself like I would never treat another person.

When I was discouraged and wanted to quit something, I attempted to motivate myself with negative self-talk: *What's the matter; are you lazy? Don't quit now, you loser!* In my preaching, I would rip every effort apart, dismissing the effectiveness of an entire sermon because of one laughable *faux pas.* If I forgot to return a phone call or otherwise failed to live up to my perfectionistic expectations, I would seethe for days.

Naturally, the more I badgered myself, the more discouraged I became. A wise friend pointed out that I was able to motivate others to greater effectiveness by offering constructive feedback wrapped in encouragement. I began to apply the same technique to myself—with amazing results.

Self-evaluation is much more than exposing my mistakes and shortcomings. It is also about celebrating when I've accomplished something I set out to do. It is recognizing and rejoicing when God uses me to make a difference. It is being grateful that I obeyed God's prompting to keep my mouth shut in a tense meeting rather than blurting out words that would have inflamed the situation. It is being aware that, although I am still far too impatient with myself, I am much more self-forgiving than I was ten years ago.

Winners who finish well evaluate their character, their progress, and their strategies relentlessly, yet don't demean themselves in the process.

CHAPTER EIGHT

Winners Beat the Battle Against Inertia

Inertia: n. 1. Physics. The tendency of a body to resist acceleration; the tendency of a body at rest to remain at rest or of a body in motion to stay in motion in a straight line unless disturbed by an external force. 2. Resistance to motion, action, or change.
—New American Heritage Dictionary

To RISK EVERYTHING ON A NEW VENTURE is always shaky; to do so at the age of seventy-five might be considered reckless by many. Not long ago I read about a man who did just that. He had inherited a fortune, then multiplied it in the field of agribusiness, becoming one of the wealthiest persons of his day. He had a beautiful home in one of the world's most desirable locations. His wife was a woman of stunning beauty and charm.

Yet he liquidated all his assets and relocated to a remote, undeveloped location, far from the cultured life he had grown accustomed to, to begin again. Just as he arrived, the area was hit by one of the worst droughts in history. He moved yet again, this time to another urban center, where he parlayed his assets and his relationships to accumulate even more wealth.

After the drought, he once again moved his entire operation to that remote location, and there began one of the most difficult and trying periods of his life. His faith, his family, and his ability to persevere were tested again and again.

Why would anyone make such dramatic changes in his life, at a time when many are content to sit back and coast?

For this man, the reason was one of obedience. God had told him, "Leave your country, your people and your father's household and go to the land I will show you" (Gen. 12:1). The man's name was Abram, and his story is a big part of the Bible's book of beginnings called Genesis.

Change Is Hard

Nothing is harder than changing the direction of your life. There are sociological forces to overcome. Educational opportunities, changes in location, and financial consequences of change all become more difficult as we grow older.

Then there are spiritual forces at work more powerful than gravity, trying to keep us from God's best for our lives. Meaningful change always involves more than an adjustment in our actions; it requires a deep-rooted change in our priorities, motives, and attitudes.

Yet millions of people appear to be waiting for life to become easy before they make the changes necessary to run the race to which they have been called. Someone noted the following comments taken from registration sheets returned to the staff of the Bridger Wilderness area:

1. Trails need to be wider so people can walk holding hands.

2. Trails need to be reconstructed. Please avoid building trails that go uphill.

3. Too many bugs and leeches and spiders and spider webs. Please spray the wilderness to rid the area of these pests.

4. Please pave the trails so they can be plowed of snow during the winter.

5. Chairlifts need to be installed in some places so we can get to wonderful views without having to hike to them.

6. The coyotes made too much noise last night and kept me awake. Please eradicate these annoying animals.

7. A small deer came into my camp and stole my jar of pickles. Is there a way I can get reimbursed?

8. Reflectors need to be placed on trees every fifty feet so people can hike at night with flashlights.

9. Escalators would help on steep uphill sections.
10. A McDonald's would be nice at the trailhead.
11. The places where trails do not exist are not well marked.
12. Too many rocks in the mountains.

Several years ago, a movie entitled *A League of Their Own* was based on the female major-league baseball teams during World War II. In one of the pivotal scenes, the star catcher of the Rockford Peaches, played by Geena Davis, threatens to quit. She's disillusioned by team management, exhausted by the travel, and worried about her husband, who has gone to war. In a low moment, she complains that the game is just "too hard."

The manager of the Rockford Peaches, played by Tom Hanks, responds, "Baseball's supposed to be hard. If it weren't hard, everybody would do it. Hard is what makes it great!"

The fact that finishing well is hard is what makes it great. To reach the eighth or ninth decade of life with your God-given dream fulfilled and your character still intact is perhaps life's greatest accomplishment. And that greatest accomplishment is the result of a lifetime full of lesser but still difficult transitions.

Anyone who has ever lost a significant amount of weight will testify that getting started is the hardest part. I have complained about my weight for at least five years. This past year, I finally became motivated to *begin*, and I dropped thirty-five pounds in four months.

Anyone who has ever made a decision to go back to school after years away from the classroom knows that looking at college catalogs and dreaming about the feelings of self-satisfaction are easy. The hard part is matriculating and being seated in a desk on that first day of class.

Anyone who has ever left a financially rewarding career to pursue a God-given dream has discovered that making a shift in the source of one's provision is challenging beyond description.

Floating or Paddling?

Why is it so hard to overcome inertia? Why do some people drift through life with no apparent direction? You'll find the answer illustrated at a nearby lake, pool, or beach. It doesn't require a lot of energy to float. In fact, floating can be relaxing. It can even take you places. Getting caught up in a current allows a person to float at a good pace. There are many rivers where people can rent tubes or canoes and float down a cool river on a hot summer day, then be picked up down river by the guide and returned to their cars.

The problem with floating is that you can't choose the direction. You either go with the current or stay in one spot. To move in a different direction or even to go against the current requires the expenditure of energy. You must begin to paddle, and paddling for any length of time is hard work.

Consider your life to this point. How did you get to where you are? Did you float, catching the current of life around you, taking the path of least resistance? Or have you had to paddle, at times upstream, to get where you are today? These questions require some time to answer.

Now consider an even bigger question: Is where you are where you want to be? More importantly, is where you are where God wants you to be?

Many Christians have become wary about their own plans and dreams. We realize our propensity toward selfish ambition and materialism, and we know that pride can be a driving factor in many of our decisions.

But Scripture assures us that as we mature in Christ, our desires gradually move from being self-focused to *God-focused*. That's why Jesus said, "If you remain in me and my words remain in you, ask whatever you wish, and it will be given you" (John 15:7). If we are deepening our relationship with God, we want the same things for our life that God does.

Examine your character, ambitions, interests, and dreams in the questions that follow, and in the process discover your focus and priorities.

Character. What must I change to become a mature believer who resembles Jesus Christ? Am I still struggling, for example, with an unwillingness to forgive someone? Is the fruit of God's Spirit (Gal. 5:22–23) evident in my life? What changes must take place in my character before my life gives evidence of him? Could the reason I am not moving closer to God's best for me be because my character is not matured to the point that I'm ready for his service?

Vision. Do I clearly know what God would have me to do? If so, what is keeping me from pursuing that vision? If not, what could be inhibiting my understanding of God's best for me? How can I keep my own ambitions from blocking that vision?

Priorities. In what areas must I invest time in order to get moving? What relationships are most important for me to carry for the rest of my life? What investments of time and relationship must I give up in order to get moving?

Costs/profits. What will I give up if I change my current lifestyle to pursue a dream? What will I gain if I pursue that dream? What do I want to leave as my legacy? Is my legacy worth giving up some things today? If not, I need a more compelling legacy.

Obstacles. Have my ambitions become my shackles? In other words, will the success I've obtained on my own blind me from the riches of God's kingdom?

Timing. In another chapter we'll discuss knowing when to make a decision. But for many, the reason we never get moving is because we always wait. Many of the opportunities that come in life require us to make a leap of faith and not wait for every detail to fall in place before we say yes to God.

Momentum

Once we have our motives clarified, once that vision is clearly defined, once we start identifying and overcoming obstacles, then we start making progress toward our goal. We have broken the hold of inertia. Slowly at first, then with a greater tempo, we start moving ahead with greater ease and results.

I've witnessed firsthand the hard work of containing forest fires. One of the early lessons hot-shot crews and smoke jumpers learn is that fire creates its own wind, and that wind can cause the fire to jump ahead much quicker than anyone can anticipate. In the same way, change creates its own powerful force. That force is called momentum. Once momentum builds in the right direction, it becomes our best friend. Without the rumbling force of momentum, we may never see the results we desire.

The Pain of an Inconsequential Life

There are two types of pain in life—the pain of self-discipline, which is always eased by accomplishment, and the pain of regret, which aches within us until we die.

Cartoon character Homer Simpson summed up the philosophy of millions when he said in a recent episode, "Kids, you tried your best and you failed miserably. The lesson is, never try." That's not exactly a philosophy to build a life around.

Over coffee one morning, I sat across from a man whom I believed had accomplished a great deal for the kingdom of God. But as we talked, he expressed a deep regret over refusing to consider a dangerous opportunity for missions service he had passed up many years earlier. "I just can't shake the notion that my life would have been far better, far more purposeful, if I had only had the courage to follow God's leading back then. Instead I took an easier path. And no matter how much I've accomplished, I just don't have the confidence that I have lived my life in a way that was God's best for me."

The greatest barrier to reaching our preferable future is seldom a lack of ability or a lack of knowledge. It is almost always a lack of will.

Self-discipline is the most important character quality we can develop. Without it, we achieve nothing significant. With it, virtually anything is possible. The greatest competition we'll ever face happens not on the battlefield, the athletic field, or in the corporate arena. It happens in our own head, between our will to discipline the mind and our mind's resistance to being disciplined.

Keeping Focused

The starting point of achievement is the desire to achieve. When we focus on our obstacles, we weaken that desire. The more we focus on our goal, the stronger our desire to reach it becomes.

One powerful way to enhance this desire is to consider frequently the consequences of our achievement. The person seeking his own fortune will focus on the effects of wealth on his life—the house he will live in, the vacations he will take.

But the Christ-follower with a kingdom agenda will focus on the joy she will experience at knowing God's pleasure and hearing "well done, good and faithful servant." Christ-followers with a kingdom agenda will focus on the lives of others who will be changed for the better and the rich legacy we'll leave to our children and subsequent generations.

We must simultaneously be both where we are, and where we are going. That's hard for any of us to do, because while the future is frequently a more compelling world than the one we're standing in, the present has a way of diverting our attention to the immediate.

This is especially important to remember when in a leadership role. If I'm living too far out in the future, I leave everyone behind. Yet I cannot give all my energy to the here and now, or I won't be able to lead. Somehow I must find the strength and courage to be there and here at the same time.

People who will most impact the kingdom of God are those who are consistently leading people toward God's best rather than settling for man's "good enough."

Beating the battle against inertia requires the ability to break a task down into bite-size pieces. Otherwise, we become demoralized by the immensity of our calling.

In writing a book, for example, I need to know exactly where this book is headed. At the same time, I've got to work on it one word, one paragraph, one page, one chapter at a time. To look at it in its entirety is exciting, but it is also intimidating. The size of the project can result in writer's block, rendering me unable to chip away at the process because the whole is too daunting.

The saying "Well begun is half done" is trite but true. Breaking free from inertia and seeing the momentum begin to build gives us hope that we can live a life fully devoted to our Lord.

CHAPTER NINE

Winners Are Still Curious About the World

Great are the works of the LORD; they are pondered
by all who delight in them.

—Psalm 111:2

As SOON AS WE LEARN TO TALK, we come up with a million questions: Why are my eyes blue? Where do babies come from? Why don't mommies have pouches like kangaroos? How much farther? How do birds fly?

Lynne Allen found herself face-to-face with one of those tough kid's questions. Her son arose one morning to discover the moon was still high in the sky, even though it was daylight. After bringing this to his mother's attention, he asked her, "Why is the moon so high?" Lynne suggested God put it up there for many reasons and then tried to give some examples. Catching his mother's spirit, the little boy looked at her and said, "Did God put it up that high so little kids can't touch it?"[11]

Curiosity is a natural response to God's presentation of his wonder and glory. To look at creation and ponder the Creator without wanting to know more is a learned behavior. Unfortunately, somewhere along the line one of two things happened to most of us.

First, someone of influence, a parent or teacher perhaps, said something along the lines of, "You ask too many questions." We became self-conscious, embarrassed, or ashamed of our curiosity. We began to stifle our questions, afraid to be singled out as one who wanted to know.

Or even worse, we reached a point where we came to believe we already had all the knowledge we really needed. Sometimes we get a warped view that says education is something to be completed so that life can then be lived.

When either of these tragedies hits us, our curiosity becomes dormant. We begin to accept the way things were without questioning. We no longer marvel at the mysteries of nature. We stop wondering about the *whats* and the *whys* and the *hows* around us.

Do you doubt what I'm saying? When was the last time you did some research, not for a project at work but simply because something intrigued you? When was the last time you looked at the stars and asked God about their mysteries? How long has it been since you looked at a child and laughed at her wide-eyed wonder?

A Necessary Skill

Some might question why curiosity would be a necessary attribute for those who want to finish well. The main reason is that without it we grow comfortable. Stagnant. Entropy sets in. We fail to recognize opportunity. We accept the status quo without questioning, "Is there a better way?"

Consider how many innovations in business were inspired by the question, "What if?" Think of all the solutions that would not have occurred had they not been sparked by a childlike curiosity. The inventions that would have remained uninvented. The books that would have remained unwritten. The friends who would have remained strangers. A curious mind is the spark that drives us to move beyond the familiar and the comfortable.

Curiosity gives us a thirst to read and learn. We frequently hear about today's rapid pace of change. Those who will thrive are those who have made a commitment to be lifelong learners. Only those who cultivate a curious spirit will experience the joy of being a student of life. Happily, our access to information makes it easy for anyone to explore virtually any topic from the comfort of his or her own living room via the Internet. Research that once took weeks can be accomplished in an afternoon.

It has never been easier to learn some basic computer skills, yet I'm amazed to meet people who are unwilling to become computer literate. These skills increase our effectiveness exponentially. Many are afraid they are too far behind the learning curve, and they will not make the effort to get "wired." Their fear overrides their curiosity, at a high price.

Curiosity asks the questions that lead to great discoveries. The inventor of Velcro got his inspiration from a walk in the woods. George de Mestral, a Swiss engineer, returned home to find some cockleburs clinging to his canvas jacket. When de Mestral pulled them free, he marveled at how the little seedpods could hold on so tenaciously. Upon examining one under a microscope, he saw each barb ended in a tiny hook. When an animal's hairy body came in contact with these hooks, a tight bond formed. The inventor saw the potential of such a bond for clothing, and began working. It took eight years of trial and error to perfect the two strips of nylon fabric, one with small loops and the other with thousands of small hooks. But the result has made life better for all of us.[12]

Curiosity keeps us from being satisfied with the status quo. Progress is always preceded by dissatisfaction. The end of every century seems to spawn a bunch of new innovations. In 1899, the director of patents for the United States government, Charles H. Duell, sent this letter to the president.

Dear Mr. President:

It is my high recommendation that you consider closing the U.S. Patent office . . . because . . . everything that could possibly be beneficial to mankind . . . has already been invented.

Curiosity opens the doors of relationships. Vernon Armitage, pastor of Pleasant Valley Church and a mentor of mine, is one of the most unassuming people I know. Although he's been in ministry for forty years, leads a church with over three thousand in attendance, and is in big demand as a speaker at conferences for pastors, he also still attends conferences and will take notes and gain insights like a rookie. I've seen him interacting with much younger pastors, asking questions about their ministries, about their lives, showing genuine interest in them. He affirms them by listening to them. He'll leave without ever once talking about his own ministry or his own success. How refreshing.

Vernon has taught me that we can make more friends in two days by being interested in others than we'll make in a year of trying to get people interested in us.

Curiosity Amplified

If a person has not retained his natural inquisitive spirit, is there anything that can be done to regain it? Happily, yes. Curiosity is another habitual attitude that can be cultivated. Here are some suggestions:

Spend time with curious people, especially children. Formal education taught us that answers are more important than questions. We frequently heard a professor ask us to hold our questions until later, so she could "get through the syllabus." An approach to education that places information above discovery inevitably leads to knowledge without context. Yet when we are in the company of people who question everything, we discover areas of our own lives that we have walled off.

When the principal of a school our children once attended died of cancer, my younger daughter asked, "Why didn't God answer our prayers and heal her?"

My first impulse was to hush her by saying, "We don't question God." Instead, we talked about how God had indeed answered our prayers by relieving her suffering and taking her home to heaven.

That triggered the next question, "What is heaven like?" Describing heaven led to a theological discussion, "Why do only those who love Jesus go to heaven?" In about five minutes, a six-year-old had managed to ask three of the most difficult questions about the Christian faith. On the inside I was thinking, *Why must you ask so many questions?* Thankfully, I didn't say that and attempted to articulate my own thoughts about these deep subjects in terms I thought she could understand.

That encounter caused me to reexamine other hard subjects I had been afraid to examine. Later that year, my senior pastor, Rick White, and I preached an eight-week sermon series entitled, "If I Could Ask God One Question." My bedtime conversation with Meagan was one of the incidents that gave rise to that series.

Keep a journal to record questions and insights. In *How to Think like Leonardo DaVinci*, Michael Gelb suggests making a list of one hundred questions. "Your list can include any kind of question as long as it's something you deem significant: anything from 'How can I save more money?' or 'How can I have more fun?' to 'What is the meaning and purpose of my existence?' and 'How can I best serve my Creator?'"[13]

Gelb recommends a hundred questions because the first twenty or so will be off the top of our heads, and it is in the next thirty or forty that themes begin to emerge. "When you have finished, read through your list and highlight the themes that emerge. Are these themes about relationships? Business? Fun? Money? The meaning of life?"

These dominant themes are more important than the actual questions, because they illuminate areas of our life where we are most open to growth and change.

Look up unfamiliar words you find while reading. Some might argue that a love for words is a symptom of a curious mind, but I believe strongly that expanding my vocabulary expands my understanding of life.

Ecclesiastes 12:9–10 says, "Not only was the Teacher wise, but also he imparted knowledge to the people. He pondered and searched out and set in order many proverbs. The Teacher searched to find just the right words, and what he wrote was upright and true."

Discovering the root of a word gives me insight into its meaning and a sense of context for its origin. For example, I first learned the word *catalyst* in chemistry and used it with a vague sense of "something that triggers an action or reaction." The word is commonly used in reference to leaders these days. We are encouraged to be catalysts for change in our arenas. We all know that change brings stress for many people, even when it is needed. So when I discovered that the Greek root of catalyst, *kata*, is also the root of *catastrophic* and *cataclysm*, I suddenly understood why I sometimes felt like I had triggered an avalanche when I had initiated change as a leader.

Learn a new language. Researchers tell us that Spanish is quickly catching up with English as the most common language in the United States. Since I have a passion to reach the thousands of Spanish-speaking new residents in my county for Christ, learning their language is going to be an essential skill.

Learning a new language also gives insight into cultural understanding. I recently learned the Spanish word for "pregnancy" is *embarazo*. That sounds a lot like our word *embarrassed*. Suddenly, this one male author had a new insight into one of the many emotions that a pregnant woman experiences, including the self-consciousness that comes from her dramatic change in appearance. This insignificant discovery led me to a much greater sensitivity than usual in a recent counseling situation with a pregnant woman.

Cultivate the art of asking for feedback. I'm curious to know what other people think, especially about the things I do that are part of my life's focus. When I teach, are people learning? When I write, do readers follow eagerly? If not, I wonder, *What can I do to improve?* I need to know, and the only way to really find out is to ask. Asking for feedback is an art, and not every person is capable of giving the kind of intentional feedback I want. So if someone comments on a study I've taught, I might ask something like, "What part made the biggest impression on you?" If they can't answer, I figure they were just being polite. If they respond, then I can probe a little, trying to discern if what they heard is remotely connected to what I intended to say.

Become a student of human nature. Why do people behave in fairly predictable ways in given circumstances? How can I learn to present new and potentially disturbing information to people without triggering their natural defense mechanisms?

Early the other morning I was flying home from a board meeting in Dallas, Texas. I had to change planes in Houston, and although my connection was tight, I was starving. I got in a long line at the terminal bakery and finally made it to the cash register with my oatmeal muffin and cup of coffee. When I handed the cashier my debit card, she pointed to a sign taped to the cash register: *We don't accept credit cards.*

"But I don't have any cash," I said, irritated by both her rudeness and her company's policy. She shrugged her shoulders and just stared at me. I just stood there, my exhausted brain unsure about what to do next.

The woman in line behind me spoke up. "Would you allow me to buy your breakfast?" she asked with a kind smile on her face.

"Oh, no. Thanks but . . ."

"Please. Let me take care of it." She turned to the cashier and said, "Add these both together." The cashier hesitated, unsure of protocol. "It's OK," the woman encouraged her. She pecked in the woman's order and announced the total.

"Thank you. Thank you so much," I told her.

She smiled again. "It is my pleasure."

On the two-hour plane ride from Houston to Nashville, I pondered this case study in human interaction. Why did the cashier act so rude about it all? Why did the woman behind me act in kindness? Why was it so hard for me to accept a considerate gesture from a stranger? These thoughts led me through a helpful process of self-discovery that would never have taken place if I hadn't cultivated an abiding interest in human behavior.

Pursue eclectic interests. Curiosity allows us to make a difference even beyond our field of expertise. How else do you explain that some famous inventions came about when people pursued an interest outside their area of training and education? John Dunlop invented the pneumatic tire, but he was a veterinarian. A cork salesman named King Gillette invented the safety razor. The founder of Kodak, George Eastman, was a bookkeeper. In 1 Corinthians 12 (NRSV), Paul uses the word *variety* three times in his discussion of spiritual gifts. We would do well to experiment more with this variety. God might use us to bring about something new in a way that surprises all of us.[14]

Take time to contemplate. Traveling at the speed of life down the twenty-first century highway, we tend to ignore most of the rest stops along the way. Our pace leaves little room for contemplating, pondering, or meditation.

We often feel guilty if we are not busy every waking hour. Because work for most of us involves our minds rather than our muscles, we "relax" by engaging in some type of mind-numbing behavior like watching television. I try so hard to maximize my time that I can unfairly categorize time set aside for thinking as "wasted time."

That's how I felt in the encounter with that kind woman in the airport. I had brought work to be done on the plane, and spending those two hours thinking about what had happened kept me from my work. But the insight I gained into my own life would never have come apart from slowing down long enough to think about it.

Luke 2:19 records the response of Mary to the dramatic events surrounding the birth of Jesus: "But Mary treasured up all these things and pondered them in her heart." While God never promises to reveal the answers to all our questions, there is much to discover when we pause long enough to reflect on his magnificent ways.

CHAPTER TEN

Winners Deal with Conflict Sooner Than Later

*"Therefore, if you are offering your gift at the altar and there
remember that your brother has something against you, leave
your gift there in front of the altar. First go and be reconciled to
your brother; then come and offer your gift."*
—Matthew 5:23–24

ANYONE WHO HAS SEEN the movie *Apocalypse Now* recalls the chilling line by the character played by Robert Duvall: "I love the smell of napalm in the morning." Napalm was a cruel but effective weapon during the Vietnam War. A jellied form of gasoline, it would stick to the skin of whoever it was dropped upon, inflicting horrible burns.

But what do you do with napalm after the war is over? The highly flammable weapon has no practical purpose.

A couple of years ago, a rail car carrying twelve thousand gallons of napalm headed back to California after political protests prompted an Indiana company to back out of a Navy deal to recycle the jellied gasoline. The Navy decided to send the shipment to China Lake Naval Weapons Testing Center, about 120 miles northwest of Los Angeles, for storage until a company was found to "treat it or process it," said Navy spokesman Lt. Comdr. John Smith.[15]

Likewise, too many people have neglected to "treat or process" the inevitable conflict that comes their way in life. The result is a relational accident waiting to happen. People abandon marriages and other valuable relationships, ministries, and careers, thinking it's easier to start over than to resolve conflict. Finishing well becomes increasingly unlikely because of the growing pile of unsettled conflicts.

One pastor I know served twelve churches in his forty years of ministry. The average stay at each was just a little over three years. Looking back on his ministry, he said:

> If I could change one thing, I'd have learned early on how to handle conflict better. My way of handling it was to find another church. When conflict arose with the deacons or the organist or just someone in the congregation who didn't like me, I would usually fail to talk it through with them face-to-face. Hoping it would go away, I'd ignore it. But it never went away. It only grew until I got so uncomfortable that I began to look for another church.
>
> The only problem was that the next church had almost the same set of problems I tried to escape in the first place. I think my ministry would have been much more effective if I had stayed in one place longer by learning to handle conflict better.

My friend is not alone. While no reasonable person likes conflict, none of us can run from it without consequence.

An Insufficient Strategy

Like that pastor, we all desperately want to believe that conflict will go away by itself. We put off confrontation and reconciliation because it can be painful, embarrassing, and risky. But the pain, embarrassment, and risk only become more pronounced when we postpone it.

Repeat the following statement until you believe it: *If I don't deal with conflict, it always grows worse instead of better.*

When ignoring conflict doesn't work, the next easiest step is to abandon the relationship. A recent societal trend enables us in our natural inclination to neglect conflict resolution. Because we move more frequently, change jobs more often, and have more options for church attendance than in years past, many have developed "disposable" relationships. We don't think that way perhaps, but our actions indicate our intentions. We rarely go below the surface in our conversations. We shelter ourselves from knowing too much about others or being known. Then, at the first hint of a disagreement, we abandon the friendship. We find a new church, move to another neighborhood, or take another job rather than go about the hard work of resolution.

Again, repeat the following statement until it sinks in: *People are not disposable.* Ditching the relationship is an indicator of spiritual immaturity.

A Better Way

Rather than trying to escape conflict, a growing person seeks to resolve it in a Christ-honoring fashion. Jesus gave some practical instruction in conflict resolution in Matthew's Gospel. "If your brother sins against you, go and show him his fault, just between the two of you. If he listens to you, you have won your brother over. But if he will not listen, take one or two others along, so that 'every matter may be established by the testimony of two or three witnesses.' If he refuses to listen to them, tell it to the church; and if he refuses to listen even to the church, treat him as you would a pagan or a tax collector" (Matt. 18:15–17).

Jesus gives us a three-step strategy to resolve interpersonal conflict. This is not some magic formula, guaranteed to solve all interpersonal disagreements. Jesus assumed that rational people want to resolve conflict. Unfortunately, some people are neither rational nor inclined to resolve the conflict! Nevertheless, things usually go much better when we seek to resolve issues God's way.

Step 1: Go One-on-One

The first step is to go directly to the person who has offended you, then tell him clearly what he has done and how that has affected you. This is contrary to what most people do when they've been hurt. Most of us tell everyone *but* the person we are angry with. How does one even begin to bring up the incident that led to the breach in fellowship? Here are some guidelines.

Stick to the issues; don't get personal. Unless you are trying to establish a pattern of behavior, don't bring up every petty grievance you have against the person.

Never assume a person's motive was to hurt you deliberately. By refusing to presume a person's intent, you avoid making judgments about his motive, so simply deal with his actions. This approach dramatically lowers the likelihood of the other person growing defensive.

Do assume a desire in your adversary's life to grow in Christlikeness. Believe your willingness to confront will help your brother or sister toward that end.

Make sure your own attitude is right before confronting anyone. Jesus told this parable in Luke 6: "Can a blind man lead a blind man? Will they not both fall into a pit? A student is not above his teacher, but everyone who is fully trained will be like his teacher. Why do you look at the speck of sawdust in your brother's eye and pay no attention to the plank in your own eye? How can you say to your brother, 'Brother, let me take the speck out of your eye,' when you yourself fail to see the plank in your own eye? You hypocrite, first take the plank out of your eye, and then you will see clearly to remove the speck from your brother's eye" (Luke 6:39–42).

Perhaps what I perceive to be an opportunity to confront someone with his or her own wrongdoing becomes an opportunity to confess my own wrongdoing.

Explain the problem simply and why it's an important issue to you. A husband who loves sports may wonder why his wife nags him continually about watching games on the weekends. If she considers it a problem and he doesn't, resolution will not happen. But if she will explain why his actions bother her, that she feels ignored when the television is on, the husband can then figure out a solution to the problem—how to make his wife feel loved, appreciated, and important.

Suggest a solution and action steps for resolving the issue. A friend of mine has developed a little phrase his staff uses in meetings to make problem-solving more effective. "Let's get on the solution side" means quit trying to assign blame and, instead, suggest a solution and figure out how to solve this effectively.

Forgive the one who has hurt you. Once the other person acknowledges her trespass, apologizes, or asks your forgiveness—or even if she doesn't—put the issue in the past. Forgiveness is refusing to hold a person's past against her and refusing to allow the past to hinder your future relationship.

Step 2: Bring in an Arbitrator

Sometimes the person who has hurt you refuses to acknowledge what she has done. In such a situation Jesus said to bring in a third party to act as a reconciler. Our tendency is to find an arbitrator who will see our side of the story, but we'll make greater headway if we seek someone who is respected by the person with whom we are at odds.

I'm greatly impressed with a company called INJOY, owned by John Maxwell. I've been able to work for this company on a number of freelance projects, and it has always been a good experience. Their standard contract for a consultant states that, should there be a dispute regarding the agreement we've entered, neither party will seek legal action, but we will take it to a mediator whose first priority is to restore unity in the relationship.

Sometimes when we are in the midst of a relational skirmish, we lose our own objectivity and try to deal with symptoms, not causes. That's why so many married couples have experienced the benefits of counseling in resolving marital issues. A neutral party can be objective and help pinpoint the real issues.

The advantages of finding an arbitrator apply in every situation. I know a senior pastor who was in perpetual conflict with a staff member. The easiest and most common thing to do in such a situation is for one person or the other to leave the church staff. Not these men. Together, they went through several sessions with a counselor to determine what the real issues were. Although the staff member did eventually leave that church, the relationship between the two was healthy as a result of their willingness to bring in a neutral party to help them sort out the conflict.

Step 3: Take the Problem to a Higher Authority

Jesus acknowledged that there are situations in which a person is either unrepentant or refuses to seek peace. In those rare cases, he taught us to bring in some authority. In a conflict in the church, it would be the church leaders. Paul took the Corinthian Christians to task for ignoring a man who was having a sexual relationship with his stepmother (1 Cor. 5:1–5). Paul said the church leaders should have confronted him out of a sense of grief that one of their own had wandered into such destructive behavior. He also told them this man should have been confronted because his own spiritual well-being was at stake. The church apparently followed Paul's instructions.

In 2 Corinthians 2:6–8, Paul may have been talking about the same situation when he told them, "The punishment inflicted on him by the majority is sufficient for him. Now instead, you ought to forgive and comfort him, so that he will not be overwhelmed by excessive sorrow. I urge you, therefore, to reaffirm your love for him."

Church discipline is rejected by many people today for several reasons. First, it is so seldom practiced today that it is completely unfamiliar to most Christians. Second, American Christians have been more influenced by the Declaration of Independence than by the Bible. We have elevated the autonomy of the individual over the good of the community. Third, we have little sense of community. When confronted with our sin, most of us will simply pack up and move to a church down the road, complaining that at our previous church, "we just weren't being fed," or "they were just so judgmental."

Certainly, spiritual leaders can be harsh and heavy-handed, but every congregation ought to consider the biblical necessity of having a plan for exercising discipline for the purpose of restoring relationships, first with God, then with one another.

This same principle is equally effective in the workplace. When two employees are unable to settle their differences, and their supervisor can't resolve the issue, sometimes it is necessary to call in a supervisor or someone from the human resources department. This sends a strong signal that resolution is not optional but essential.

While profits often matter more than relationships in many organizations today, the wise leader can show that healthy relationships increase profitability and that putting a priority on restoring relationships makes good fiscal sense. Christians in positions of leadership can implement this biblical strategy for conflict resolution without mentioning that it came from Jesus.

In some extreme situations, the principle of appealing to a higher authority may mean it is necessary to involve law enforcement. Raynelle was in a difficult marriage, one in which her husband would occasionally binge on alcohol and become verbally abusive. She would confront him the next morning when he was sober again, and they had counseled with their pastor on several occasions. He was always remorseful and would go long periods between binges, but inevitably he would succumb again. Finally, after he slapped her while drunk, she called the police and had him arrested and kept in jail overnight. The shame and shock of that event was the catalyst for him to enter counseling for his alcoholism. He never drank or hit her again.

If, after going through these sequential processes, a person is still unrepentant or unwilling to resolve the issue, according to Jesus the relationship should be severed, and the person who won't reconcile should be avoided. Such extreme measures should be for extreme situations. Unfortunately, this is often the first thing we do when conflict interrupts our lives.

When the Shoe Is on the Other Foot

I've had the uncomfortable opportunity to be on the other end when a mature Christian has come to me and said, "Ed, you may not be aware of this, but I'm having a hard time keeping a healthy attitude toward you because of . . ." In most cases, I was not even aware that I had hurt that person. Other times, something I said had been misunderstood or misinterpreted. I was able to express regret that I had hurt my brother or sister in Christ and to clarify what I meant to say.

But sometimes I was deliberately rude or critical or sarcastic with someone, and their confrontation was the catalyst I needed to confess my sin to God and repent. Proverbs says, "He who rebukes a man will in the end gain more favor than he who has a flattering tongue" (Prov. 28:23).

The Bible also provides us with practical preventive steps which, when incorporated into our normal interaction, go a long way toward reducing conflict in the first place.

Listen more than you talk. "He who answers before listening— that is his folly and his shame" (Prov. 18:13).

Speak the truth in love. "Instead, speaking the truth in love, we will in all things grow up into him who is the Head, that is, Christ" (Eph. 4:15).

Don't allow anger to rule your life. "'In your anger, do not sin': Do not let the sun go down while you are still angry, and do not give the devil a foothold" (Eph. 4:26–27).

Admit when you are wrong. "The way of a fool seems right to him, but a wise man listens to advice" (Prov. 12:15).

Americans are lonelier than ever before. We want relationships, but we don't want to work at them. Becoming a person who deals promptly and biblically with conflict will help ensure that we will look back upon our lives one day and reflect upon the rich blessings that have come our way through people. Our spouses, children, friends, business associates, neighbors, pastors, Sunday school teachers, and brothers and sisters in Christ will all help us become the man or woman God created us to be—if we will allow them to confront us and save us from ourselves.

CHAPTER ELEVEN

Winners Keep Anger from Accumulating

"Repent of this wickedness and pray to the Lord. Perhaps he will forgive you for having such a thought in your heart. For I see that you are full of bitterness and captive to sin."
—Acts 8:22–23

DURING A RECENT BAPTISM, I paraphrased a passage of Scripture to fit the situation: "If anyone is in Christ, he *or she* (I was baptizing a young woman) is a new creature in Christ."

The next morning I was going through the communication cards we use for guest registration, prayer requests, and miscellaneous information. One of the critical cards that week took me to task for "daring to change the infallible, inerrant, unchangeable Word of God. When the Bible says 'he' it means 'he' . . . to change it to fit *a rampant feminist agenda* is the worst kind of heresy."

Most Monday mornings, I would have tossed it in the trash with the hope that he would take a laxative and feel better. But that particular Monday, I was already cranky for reasons I cannot remember, and his note really scorched me. I wasted an hour or more writing a scathing reply, even though the note was unsigned. (We've since adopted the policy of trashing unsigned critiques without reading them.)

At lunch I told a buddy on staff about it, and he asked, "Why did that one make you so angry?"

"I don't know," I grumped. "I'm sick of stupid people and their stupid comments and their stupid inability to rejoice that someone made a public declaration of their faith. I'd like to show him a little heresy right across the jaw."

"Got a little anger problem there, don't you?" he asked.

"Of course not. It ticks me off that you'd even mention it."

I eventually admitted he was right, and we talked it through. We both agreed that over the past few years, anger arrives a little sooner and stays a little longer than we like. Petty issues that would once have received only a fleeting thought now get under our skins, where they fester. Imaginary conversations with those we are angry with get nasty or even violent.

What's up? Do most people grow angrier with every passing year, or are my friend and I just in need of a good therapist?

Causes

Life as an adult is far more complex than we ever imagined. So many of the people around us are living with pain and discouragement that they lash out at those around them. You've heard it before—*hurting people hurt people.* But the reasons for a growing anger go far deeper

More responsibility, less support. When we were children, we had far less responsibility and far more support with the details of life. On a recent vacation, I watched my seven-year-old daughter lying on her back looking for animal shapes in the clouds. *She hasn't a care in the world,* I thought, wondering when was the last time I had felt free from the responsibilities of life. I realized that often my anger stems from my need for help when it feels like no one is there to give me a hand.

Certainly I'm aware that God is in control and the church I serve belongs to him. Still, I feel this awesome responsibility to be a part of transforming a world increasingly hostile to the gospel, and sometimes the people who are supposed to help carry out the Great Commission become the very obstacles we must overcome to reach that world. People with a casual faith, blinded by the incipient universalism of our day, don't make good evangelists.

Accumulation of petty grievances. When I was a young boy, a neighboring family came down with a devastating illness. Several of the children died, and the rest suffered permanent brain damage. Investigators discovered that the father had found a truckload of discarded seed corn and fed it to the family hogs. The corn (not intended for animal feed) had been treated with something so insects wouldn't eat it before it germinated. The hogs ate it, seemingly with no ill effects.

But when the family hogs became the family breakfast, the family was poisoned. It seems that many substances like pesticides, and heavy metals like lead and mercury, do not pass through the digestive system but remain in the body—always. In tiny doses, the effects are minimal. But over time, the effects are horrible.

That's what happens to many of us in life. Every day we ingest minute amounts of conflict and disrespect at work, at home, even at church. *No big deal,* we think. *Just blow it off!* But we don't. Instead it gets buried in our liver. Twenty years later, we go ballistic when some idiot cuts us off in traffic, and then we wonder, *Gee, where did that come from?*

Dissonance between expectation and reality. We all have expectations for life—expectations for marriage, for our lifestyle, for our careers. In many cases those expectations are based on speculation at best, sheer fantasy at worst. Yet we don't know that, so as life unfolds for us quite differently than we imagined it, we grow increasingly annoyed, then disappointed, and even bitter.

My pastor friend George Clark says, "Midlife is when the skepticism of youth collides with the cynicism of old age." By the time we gain enough experience to be wise, we have also picked up enough battle wounds to be angry. Our best years of service to God could be in our fifties and sixties, but far too many professing Christians have grown so tired and self-focused by that age that they drop out of service altogether. I'm not just speaking about serving in their church, but in all of life. Why is that?

In many cases, it's the result of disappointment. Most of us never attain some unspoken goals. Perhaps it's the expectation for a comfortable income or a particular size or style of home. We never make it to the top of our profession. The invitations from book publishers and conference planners still aren't coming, and our alma mater still hasn't honored us as alumnus of the millennium. Coming to terms with unrealized dreams and goals is part of our maturation process. Often, when we scuttle our dreams, God gives us a better one.

Partial Solutions

Pick up most any magazine in the rack at the grocery store and you'll find an article about supposed solutions to inappropriate anger. *Go easy on yourself. Find a hobby that helps you relax. Get more exercise. Get more sleep. Get a pet. Bladdy bladdy blah.* The fact that the dog messed on the carpet, I don't have time for a hobby, or I don't get enough exercise or restful sleep is part of the reason I'm angry in the first place.

Truth be told, unresolved anger is a spiritual problem that won't get better without a spiritual solution.

Better Solutions

Discover why I need to be busy all the time. When I overbook my life, I get stressed. When I get stressed, I get insomnia. When I get insomnia, I get cranky. "So why not just work fewer hours?" some uninformed person might ask. Because I have to, that's why. Why? *I hate digging too deep into motives. Too often I find they are only partly true at best and, at worst, irrational.*

Because most days I enjoy my work. *True.* Because my colleagues and family members are counting on me for leadership. *Mostly true.* Because the fate of the world depends on me. *Really? And just what role does God play here?* And because there are voices from my past telling me, "You're lazy," or "You'll never amount to anything." *How sad is that, to live life today based on comments from thirty years ago?*

It's not just being busy with work that gets to us. I found myself feeling resentful last Thursday night because I had to coach my daughter's basketball team. I love my daughter and her teammates, but that night I needed solitude more than anything.

And here's another stressor. I feel selfish for taking time away from my family to spend time by myself. Even my quiet time alone with God feels like work when I get out of alignment. Anger is a by-product of a life with skewed priorities.

Jesus modeled for us a rhythm of periodically retreating from both people and process long enough to recharge. Jesus said to his weary disciples, "Come with me by yourselves to a quiet place and get some rest" (Mark 6:31). When I read that, I found myself thinking, *I wish someone would say that to me.* It took a while to realize that he did and does.

When we're used to living with the pedal to the metal, allowing ourselves to idle feels pretty uncomfortable. But it's necessary if we want to get a grip on our anger.

Give more than lip service to the necessity of community. Someone has said that the only two organizations that are really changing people are twelve-step groups and the church. The common denominator behind the success of both is community. Change happens when we allow others into our lives.

It's hard to build deep, trustworthy friendships in today's shallow social climate. Men in particular seem to have trouble letting others get close to us. But let's just get over it. You and I desperately need some people in our lives who will attempt to love us unconditionally, who know us well enough to know when we are hiding something, who can get away with confronting us, and who can "spur [us] on toward love and good deeds" (Heb. 10:24). As hard as it may be to connect with others, we'll never get our anger under control alone. I can choose to seethe in solitude or to change in community.

Give up the occupation of people-pleasing. A friend recently experienced a rebirth of sorts in his ministry. When I asked him what had happened, he responded, "After a dozen years in ministry I discovered it wasn't my job to make or keep people happy."

Pursuing purpose instead of popularity allows me to keep focused in spite of criticism. If people don't like me, it makes me sad (after all, what's not to like?), but it no longer angers me. As long as my life is invested in pleasing God, as long as the ones who know me best love me most, I can deal with rejection from the masses.

Letting go of unresolved hurts. A man came to see me a while back. He said it was to talk about membership in our church. As we talked, he began to tell me how his wife had left him over a decade ago for a love affair with another woman. As he talked, his face grew flushed, a vein popped out on his forehead, and his voice grew louder and more strident. It was apparent that he was no closer to being free from this painful event after ten years than he had been the day he found out she was leaving.

When I asked if he had forgiven her, he exploded. "Forgive her? After what she's done to me? I'll never forgive her. I'll never let her off the hook. I'd rather die than forgive her."

Forgiveness is the harder road, and one that must be taken intentionally. Living our lives on cruise control will always take us down the interstate of bitterness. I've found that I must consciously forgive even the slightest of slights if I am to maintain good emotional health.

Paul reminds us that it's helpful to reflect on all that God has forgiven us of: "Be kind and compassionate to one another, forgiving each other, just as in Christ God forgave you" (Eph. 4:32).

When to See a Professional

Sometimes anger builds to such a toxic level that we are unable to purge ourselves of it without help from a therapist or counselor. When do I call for some help?

When I feel the need to react with violence. In this day of disgruntled postal workers and disenfranchised students who take guns to school, we see the extent to which angry people will react. And while few of us would ever physically shoot someone, we entertain fantasies of verbal, even physical, violence. We carry on fantasy arguments with our bosses, our spouses, our customers, and each version becomes more caustic and bitter. These fantasies are evidence of strong anger—anger that may not go away even if that imaginary conversation became real.

When I seriously contemplate running away from it all. How many of your friends have called it quits in their marriage? How many have given up their ministries or careers because they couldn't handle the accumulation of anger and resulting bitterness? For me, the answer is too many.

Walking away from your ministry, your family, or your future is a decision no one should make without wise counsel from someone who is equipped to help you get to the root of the issues.

When anger poisons my best relationships. It was one of those days. A parishioner didn't show up for our six o'clock breakfast meeting after he had insisted we meet as soon as possible. An early morning phone call made it apparent that the chair of our properties committee had lied to me about the expense and time required for some much-needed repairs on our building. An anonymous letter not only criticized my last sermon but also my motives and devotion to God. The computer was doing things it was not supposed to. This was all before noon.

When I got home for a quick bite of lunch, a tricycle blocked my side of the driveway. Guess who got the brunt of my smoldering anger? A sweet, little four-year-old who came running out of the house to greet her daddy. The intensity of my outburst was a wake-up call for me. I started driving halfway across the state every other Monday to see a counselor.

I insisted the problem was "them." He hung in there long enough to convince me that the building rage within me was *my* problem. In the long run the ones who stood the greatest chance of being hurt by it were not "them." Once I accepted the problem as my own, that put me in control to do something about it.

As I enter the middle years of this race called life, I struggle to throw off some ugly souvenirs of anger I picked up along the way. I'm more committed than ever to finishing this race with my faith, character, and family intact. I refuse to allow anger to rob me of experiencing joy along the way. And I reject the notion that change is too hard, or that it's optional. With the help of my small group, my family, and the Holy Spirit who resides within me, I'm hopeful that I'll finish the race with no residual effects from the anger that has hindered me thus far.

CHAPTER TWELVE

Winners Make Worry Work for Them

"Martha, Martha," the Lord answered, "you are worried and upset about many things, but only one thing is needed."
—Luke 10:41–42a

ONE OF THE PASTORS I INTERVIEWED in preparing for this book revealed a painful secret from one of his early pastorates. "I worried myself right into a nervous breakdown," he said. "I worried about the already-evident conflict in my new church. I was worried because my children were struggling to adjust to a new home and new schools. I worried about how we were going to make ends meet on such a meager salary. I worried to the point that I couldn't even pray about these things anymore. That was the beginning of the end."

He was hospitalized after his wife found him in the bathroom, arms wrapped around his knees, sobbing uncontrollably. He spent a month under heavy sedation, was subjected to electroshock therapy and was out of ministry for almost a year. His church terminated him while he was hospitalized. After he began healing, he was forced to uproot his family in search of a place to serve. It took almost twelve years for his family to recover financially.

This pastor eventually recovered and went on to another three decades of successful ministry because he was willing to replace the negative thought patterns with better ones than those which had governed his emotional life up to that watershed event. While his story may be a bit dramatic, it highlights the destructive power of worry.

The poet Robert Frost wrote, "The reason why worry kills more people than work is that more people worry than work." The word *worry* comes from an old Anglo-Saxon word that means "to choke" or "to strangle." That's an apt description of what worry does to us. Worry won't stretch our savings account, bring back that prodigal son or daughter, or keep cancer or senility at bay.

But it will cause us to lose sleep. It will give us ulcers and high blood pressure and headaches. It will sour our mood and distance our friends and eventually stifle our relationship with God. It not only has physical consequences; it has spiritual consequences as well.

Worry Roots

Worry is the anxiety caused when we think we might lose something that is important to us. Sometimes it's obvious. "I'm worried about losing my job." "I'm worried about losing my spouse." "I'm worried that I'm losing my mind."

At other times your potential loss is a little trickier to identify. You are afraid because you are losing the ability to control your situation. You are anxious about the future and realize you are afraid of losing a dream.

Maybe your real fear is not losing a job. You may hate your job. What you are afraid of losing is the lifestyle you've come to enjoy and expect. Maybe you are afraid that if you lose your job, others may discover that you are not as perfect as you have marketed yourself to be.

Discovering what real loss is at stake allows you to become more specific at seeking solutions—or it highlights just how irrational your worry has become.

Worriers come in many shapes and sizes. Some are casual worriers; it is more of a hobby. Others have become full-time professionals at this deadly game.

Mayday worriers. Life is full of risks. Weighing risk is an important part of decision making. But scaring ourselves by dwelling on remote or unlikely risks and anticipating the worst-case scenario in every situation is a surefire perscription for sleepless nights and anxious days. Mayday worriers continually live as if their plane is going down and no one is responding on the radio.

Yesterday worriers. These are the people who cannot get past their mistakes of the past. They suffer from the "shoulda-coulda-woulda syndrome." "I shoulda known I was about to get fired." "I coulda had my résumé out earlier." "I woulda pursued that other lead."

The events of yesterday can give us the wisdom to make better choices today, but none of us possess the power to take back a careless word, undo a careless act, or unthink a sinful thought. Yesterday worrying is perhaps the most futile category.

Someday worriers. Speculation about what might happen is futile. Tomorrow belongs to God. It is completely his, with all its possibilities, burdens, perils, promise, and potential. It may be mine in time, but for right now, it is his. Therefore I will not worry about what is not even mine yet.

Everyday worriers. Some people get trapped in a cycle of worry, replaying the same scenario over and over. They lie awake all night and literally worry themselves sick. For these people, worry has moved from a hobby to a full-time occupation.

An Alternative: Creative Anxiety

To worry about things we cannot change is a terrible waste of emotional energy. To worry about things we can change is a terrible waste of time. Rather than worry, people who go the distance have learned instead the art of "creative anxiety."

While worry is destructive, creative anxiety is constructive. Worry focuses us on the problem; creative anxiety focuses on solutions. Worry controls us; creative anxiety puts us in control of our emotions. Here are some ways to drop the worry habit and learn new patterns of thinking.

Schedule creative anxiety. Worry creates a false sense of urgency. We find freedom from worry, then, by identifying that false urgency and making plans to consider options and solutions in a more appropriate time. Setting some personal parameters is helpful, such as: I won't worry about work on personal time. I won't worry about family when I'm working. I won't worry about unlikely possibilities until they become probable.

Ever had the experience of lying awake unable to sleep because of some nagging problem that begs to be resolved immediately? By keeping paper and pencil next to my bed, I can capture that thought and then rest knowing that I'll deal with it tomorrow.

The next morning, the optimistic light of day often causes a problem to lose its ominous shadow, and I trash the note. But if the item still seems important, I find a blank spot in my personal planner and schedule a time to deal with it then. By the time that appointment with my worry comes, one of three possibilities has emerged:

1.　The problem has resolved itself.
2.　I'm fresh and creative and can figure out a solution.
3.　I say, "I'm too busy to worry about something silly like this." You know from experience how things that get delayed often get dropped. I'm learning to kill a lot of my worries from sheer neglect.

Think the concern through, then set it aside. Regardless of our profession, most people have parts of their work that cannot be completed in one block of time. Preparing a sermon takes several blocks of time from one Sunday to the next. A business proposal is the result of research, numerous meetings, consultations, and revisions. In the same way, acknowledging that we may not solve life's great problems in one sitting can be a liberating thought. Work it through; even create a file folder with notes and doodles and possible solutions. Then you can park your anxiety in that folder until you come back to it.

Imagining positive possibilities. Creative thinking means postponing judgment on an idea for another day. Instead of saying it won't work, consider all solutions as possibilities, regardless of how far-fetched they may seem. We do serve a God who knows no limitations.

Part of what makes creative anxiety work is the willingness to look for less-than-obvious solutions.

Give yourself permission to be less than perfect. Most small children do not waste a second on worry. Those who do are usually identified by a parent or teacher as having a streak of perfectionism. I said earlier that all our worries are rooted in fear of loss. What many people fear is losing their inaccurate self-portrait of having it all together.

Perfectionists (speaking as one afflicted with this shortcoming) would rather postpone something than see it done less than perfectly. This habitual postponement causes great anxiety and leads to worrisome habits.

Practice the discipline of submission. Part of our old nature is the desire to control. We want to control our circumstances, our relationships, our future. People with a high need to control are often labeled "control freaks" by those around them.

Control freaks are prime candidates for worry-rooted disorders because so much of life is beyond our control. When something like cancer, downsizing, a lawsuit, or a rebel adolescent enters our lives, those who need to control go into a tailspin.

The issue of control is at the heart of one of the most significant passages in all the New Testament. "Your attitude should be the same as that of Christ Jesus: Who, being in very nature God, did not consider equality with God something to be grasped, but made himself nothing, taking the very nature of a *servant*" (Phil. 2:5–7, emphasis added).

Servants are never in control. They are submitted to their master. Jesus gave up control—of the universe—in order that he might please his Father and redeem humankind.

When we fully understand our relationship to God and assume the role of servant, we leave behind the need to control and the worry that tags along with that need. It is our doubt that God will provide that keeps us from releasing control. Jesus knew about this universal tendency to doubt God's intent to provide for us.

> Jesus said to his disciples: "Therefore I tell you, do not worry about your life, what you will eat; or about your body, what you will wear. Life is more than food, and the body more than clothes. Consider the ravens: They do not sow or reap; they have no storeroom or barn; yet God feeds them. And how much more valuable you are than birds! Who of you by worrying can add a single hour to his life? Since you cannot do this very little thing, why do you worry about the rest?
>
> "Consider how the lilies grow. They do not labor or spin. Yet I tell you, not even Solomon in all his splendor was dressed like one of these. If that is how God clothes the grass of the field, which is here today, and tomorrow is thrown into the fire, how much more will he clothe you, O you of little faith! And do not set your heart on what you will eat or drink; do not worry about it. For the pagan world runs after all such things, and your Father knows that you need them. But seek his kingdom, and these things will be given to you as well" (Luke 12:22–31).

Jesus offered help for worriers by reminding us of three important truths.

1. We are of infinite worth to God. Here we identify what is perhaps our greatest stumbling block. At one time or another, many have heard from a parent or sibling, teacher, minister, employer, or spouse the message, "You are unlovable."

Words like, "Can't you do anything right?" or "Why can't you be more like your sister?" or "What's wrong with you anyway?" or "I've found someone else" erode our sense of value until we start to doubt whether even God could love us.

All creation is of great value to its Creator. God's provision for his lesser creations—birds and flowers in this illustration—gives us assurance that he will not neglect those who have been made in his own image. Our worth in God's eyes is best demonstrated in that keystone verse of the New Testament: "For God so loved the world that he gave his one and only Son, that whoever believes in him shall not perish but have eternal life" (John 3:16).

The one who knows us best will, in all things, guide us toward his preferable future for our lives.

2. Worry is futile. Jesus offers a simple test: Can worry add a single hour to your life? No. In fact, worry will most likely subtract hours from it instead. Worry has no productive value. Worry is an indicator of our level of faith and trust in God. Whenever we choose to worry about something, we are in effect saying, "I'm not sure God will do anything about my situation."

Once we identify worry as a lack of trust, then we can turn it over to God. Verses like Isaiah 26:3 get us back on track: "You will keep in perfect peace him whose mind is steadfast, because he trusts in you."

Trust or faith is the essential ingredient in an authentic relationship with Jesus. Putting our future in his hands—all of our future—is the mark of a Christ-follower.

3. True wealth cannot be held in our hands. A close look at our checkbooks and our calendar reveal our true priorities. The way we spend our time and our money says it all. There is little visible difference between the priorities of today's American Christian and his unbelieving neighbor. Both live in as big a house as they can afford. Both contribute about the same stingy amount to charitable institutions. Both live from paycheck to paycheck. And both spend most of their time worrying about wanting stuff, paying for that stuff, and hanging on to their stuff.

While our concern is almost always for the things of this world, our Father's greatest desire is to give us kingdom wealth. When we refocus our vision of wealth, we realize the extent to which God provides for us, both in this life and in the life to come.

Those things that are of ultimate value cannot be lost—our salvation and the lives we influence for God's kingdom. These are the things that thieves can't steal and moths can't destroy.

A popular bumper sticker on many recreational vehicles reads, "RETIRED: No job, no responsibilities, no worries." If only that last part were true for everyone. For those who want to finish well at life, giving up the debilitating influence of worry is one big step toward a life well lived.

CHAPTER THIRTEEN

Winners Don't Live to Be Liked

"I was afraid of the people and so I gave in to them."
—1 Samuel 15:24

THERE ARE VERY FEW PEOPLE who truly don't care what other people think about them.

I was speaking at a church in the Chicago area several years ago. During my message I noticed two older women off to my right who seemed focused on every word. Dressed immaculately, white hair coifed to perfection, they both maintained eye contact, smiled at me frequently, and scribbled copious notes. They even leaned over and whispered to each other after a particularly brilliant insight.

Their attentiveness was in such contrast to the rest of the congregation that I slowly but surely began speaking to an audience of two. They laughed at every attempt at humor, nodded knowingly when I quoted a favorite theologian, and gave me a sense of self-confidence that a guest speaker struggles to find in a strange location. I became convinced that there had never been a more powerful sermon preached and that these ladies had never received such a spiritual blessing. Surely the Holy Spirit was moving among us.

After the service, I stood by the exit with the pastor, who introduced me to his congregation as they walked by. Shaking hands with everyone, I received the obligatory, "Thanks for coming," and "That was a nice sermon," but all the while I was looking for the two white-haired ladies, anxious to hear their praise.

They were the last two in line. I thought I heard the pastor mutter something under his breath as they approached, but I ignored him. I was about to meet the future officers of my own fan club.

The spokeswoman for the pair clasped my hand and smiled up at me, her faded blue eyes flashing. I made a mental note to act humbly, no matter how lavish the praise. "My sister and I couldn't help but wonder the whole time you were preaching," she said. "Is that your real hair?" With that they both laughed.

My mouth moved, but no sound came out. My brain scrambled to decipher this strange question that did not fit at all with where I thought she was going. *Where was the praise? Where was the gratitude?* Before I could get a word out, the other sister said, "I told her it had to be real; no man would buy a skull rug that looked that coarse."

As they laughed yet again, it dawned on me what the smiles and the whispers had been about. The pastor inserted himself between us and hustled the old girls out the door. He walked back shaking his head. "I'm sorry. I should have warned you. Rachel and Diana are a little odd."

Still in shock, I whispered to no one in particular, "It, it really is my hair."

Though that has since become one of my favorite stories, I was wounded by their words for a while. For months after that incident I wondered every time I stood up to speak, *Are they laughing at my hair?* What really bothered me was how quickly I had allowed the attention of those women to influence my speaking. Why had that happened? I wanted to be liked.

Someone asked comedian Bill Cosby to define the secret to success. "I don't know the secret to success, but I do know the secret to failure—trying to please everyone."

Roots of People-Pleasing

We learn as small children that pleasing others brings rewards. *If I clean up my plate, Mom will praise me and give me dessert. If I bring home good grades, I may be rewarded.*

That cause-and-effect behavior carries over to adulthood. *If I stay late and finish a report on time, the boss will remember my dedication come promotion time. If I help my wife with the dishes or bathe the kids, she will be more relaxed and inclined toward intimacy at bedtime.*

Politicians are sometimes accused of "leading by the polls." If the polls indicate that the majority holds a particular opinion, then the politician embraces that opinion—at least until public opinion swings another way. This policy can get a candidate elected once or twice, but after a while Americans quit voting for someone who holds no convictions of his own.

At some point, a healthy desire to see people we love experience joy gives way to something unhealthy. We all are tempted at some point to do things we know are wrong in order to be liked. A child steals, drinks, or smokes to gain approval from her peers. A pastor neglects his family to please his parishioners. An ad executive approves a commercial that blatantly misrepresents the product in order to please a client.

It's often a question of motive. The same action can be right or wrong, depending on the motive behind it. Working overtime can be a necessity of any job from time to time. But it can easily become an alternative to going home to a tense atmosphere where a marriage is slowly choking to death. Working overtime can also be a means of seeking praise from my peers or my managers in order to satisfy my insecurities. Or work can even become an obsession or addiction, in which case enough is never enough.

How can I know the purity of my motive? To some extent, I never can. And yet, if I earnestly desire to know my motives, God is faithful to reveal them. I can begin by asking myself some hard questions: Am I motivated to do this more by my own insecurity than by a desire to serve another person? Am I afraid of being rejected if I say no? Am I expecting to receive something in return? Did I determine my course of action based on what is popular, not what is right?

Pleasing those we love is rewarding, and this may not be wrong in and of itself. But pleasing God is a higher calling and much more fulfilling. We are headed for trouble when our desire to please people and gain their approval becomes as important as pleasing God and sensing his approval.

This doesn't mean we don't treat others well and strive to be likable in our personality. Rather, it means that our most important decisions are not motivated by the unhealthy need to win the approval of others.

Poet e. e. cummings wrote, "To be nobody but yourself—in a world which is doing its best, night and day, to make you everybody else—means to fight the hardest battle which any human can fight, and never stop fighting."

Perils of People-Pleasing

Being a people-pleaser will affect your relationship with God. The Bible is full of illustrations of what happens when pleasing people becomes our focus. Jesus warned us of the danger of wrong motives.

"I do not accept praise from men, but I know you. I know that you do not have the love of God in your hearts. I have come in my Father's name, and you do not accept me; but if someone else comes in his own name, you will accept him. How can you believe if you accept praise from one another, yet make no effort to obtain the praise that comes from the only God?" (John 5:41–44).

Paul echoed those words when he wrote the church in Galatia: "Am I now trying to win the approval of men, or of God? Or am I trying to please men? If I were still trying to please men, I would not be a servant of Christ" (Gal. 1:10).

God has required absolute fidelity from his people. Our response to that requirement comes easily when we keep focused on the extent of God's love for us. When our insecurities drive us to seek the approval of others, we lose sight of all he has done on our behalf.

Being a people-pleaser will affect your ability to make good decisions. Every parent has known the tension of having to say no to an activity their child desperately wanted to attend. A sleepover at a home where adult supervision will be lacking, attending a concert that may contain inappropriate material, wanting to take on one too many extracurricular activities—telling your children they cannot participate in any of these will lead to their disappointment and even anger. Parents who are prone to people-pleasing will find themselves compromising their own good judgment just to keep their children happy.

Business leaders can face the same dilemma—make the right call that is best for the overall health of the company, or make the easier decision that will make the influential people happy. It happened to a biblical leader: "Then Saul [first king of Israel] said to Samuel, 'I have sinned. I violated the LORD's command and your instructions. I was afraid of the people and so I gave in to them'" (1 Sam. 15:24).

Being a people-pleaser can make people uncomfortable around you. An overeager personality craves an inordinate amount of feedback. Every task, no matter how small, demands a response. "Did I do this OK? If it isn't the way you want it, I can do it again. Just let me know." *Yep, that photocopy looks just fine.*

A spouse who needs constant affirmation because of his insecurity will slowly but surely stifle his marriage. An "I love you" becomes not a declaration of affection but the prompt to hear the other say, "I love you too."

Being a people-pleaser will wear you out. I shared in an earlier chapter about a fellow pastor who found great freedom when he discovered "it wasn't my job to keep everyone happy anymore." Whether you are a pastor, a manager, a mother, or a small-group leader, there are few burdens heavier than that of carrying the responsibility for everyone's happiness.

The Antidote

The people-pleaser must eventually come to terms with two truths:

Not everyone will love me. I've struggled to understand this truth in my own life. Yet I've discovered that some people will instantly dislike me because I'm a pastor. Others find I remind them of someone they don't like, so they don't like me either. The reasons are many and are often irrational. Romans 12:18 has helped me understand that I can only do so much: "If it is possible, as far as it depends on you, live at peace with everyone." If I've done my part to maintain a healthy relationship, I let go of any expectation on the part of another person.

Those who do love me will never love me the way I crave to be loved. Human love is multifaceted, and it is a wonderful thing to experience. And yet it is imperfect and often falls short of the biblical ideal of unconditional love. What the people-pleaser longs for is unending acceptance and affirmation. No person can feed that insatiable appetite. But God can.

The only real freedom for people-pleasers comes from understanding and experiencing security in our relationship with God and who we are in Christ.

The Nature of Our Relationship with God

People-pleasers live in fear that others will learn of their past failures, mistakes, and shortcomings and therefore will choose not to love them. We are all haunted occasionally by a painful episode from the past that humiliates and embarrasses us. If only we could wipe the slate clean and become something more than our lifetime accumulation of sin and failure.

Second Corinthians 5:17–19 says, "Therefore, if anyone is in Christ, he is a new creation; the old has gone, the new has come! All this is from God, who reconciled us to himself through Christ and gave us the ministry of reconciliation: that God was reconciling the world to himself in Christ, not counting men's sins against them. And he has committed to us the message of reconciliation."

At one time, our sin nature kept us separated from God. But when we receive Jesus Christ, "to all who received him, to those who believed in his name, he gave the right to become *children of God*" (John 1:12, emphasis added).

Another insight into our new relationship with God is found in John 15:15 when Jesus makes a startling statement to his disciples: "I no longer call you servants, because a servant does not know his master's business. Instead, I have called you *friends*, for everything that I learned from my Father I have made known to you" (emphasis added). Even more startling is the fact that Jesus' declaration extends to all his disciples, including you and me.

The Implications of That Relationship

We too often fail to grasp the implications of these verses. We have a clean slate from which to go forward with life. Since we are God's children, all that is his becomes ours. We have all the resources of God's kingdom available to us. And as Jesus' friends, we have the possibility of developing the greatest relationship we can ever know. Ephesians 1:7–8 summarizes what this means: "In him we have redemption through his blood, the forgiveness of sins, in accordance with the riches of God's grace that he lavished on us with all wisdom and understanding."

We are no longer separated from God by our sin and rebellion. Jesus serves as our bridge to God. Ephesians 2:18 tells us, "For through him we both have access to the Father by one Spirit."

And 2 Peter 1:3–4 gives us a glimpse of how our relationship with Jesus can lift us to a new plain of living. "His divine power has given us everything we need for life and godliness through our knowledge of him who called us by his own glory and goodness. Through these he has given us his very great and precious promises, so that through them you may participate in the divine nature and escape the corruption in the world caused by evil desires."

Once we are secure in our relationship with God and understand the implications of that relationship, we seek to know how we can please him. Jesus explained to his disciples that loving God was demonstrated by obeying God (John 14:21).

The Worship Connection

I've struggled to know God's love, emotionally not intellectually. I believe the Bible, and the message of God's love for us is the Bible's dominant theme. God's love is the heart of the gospel that I preach. I know this both intellectually and through faith.

My struggle and the secret struggle of many Christians is not with the head but with the heart. God's love had to become experiential before I could give up people-pleasing.

God's love became tangible for me through worship. By *worship*, I do not mean singing religious songs in a church meeting, though worship can certainly occur there. Our church defines it this way: "Genuine worship is responding in love with all that I am—mind, emotions, will and body—to all that God has done and said in the past, and is doing and saying today." Our goal is to lead people to transcendent encounters with God. Those transcendent encounters have virtually liberated me from the need to impress others. It's ironic that while expressing my love for God, I have most experienced God's love for me. And nothing satisfies more.

The ancient Irish hymn *Be Thou My Vision* is one of thousands of songs that speak of the joy of putting God's favor ahead of all else.

> Riches I heed not, or man's empty praise,
> Thou mine inheritance, now and always:
> Thou and thou only, first in my heart,
> High King of heaven, my treasure thou art.

That's the song of my heart as well.

CHAPTER FOURTEEN

Winners Have Learned to Say No

*After the people saw the miraculous sign that Jesus did, they
began to say, "Surely this is the Prophet who is to come into the
world." Jesus, knowing that they intended to come and make him
king by force, withdrew again to a mountain by himself.*
—John 6:14–15

THE SUMMER OF 2000 was a nightmare for many air travelers.
More flights were delayed or cancelled than at any other time in
history. Airlines overbooked flights, and airports scheduled too
many flights, leaving thousands of passengers stranded in airports around the country. A commercial for United Airlines fea-
tured their president, James E. Goodwin, apologizing to the
American people. Mr. Goodwin pledged his company's commitment to quit overbooking flights and to begin posting more
realistic departure and arrival times.

Some days my life feels like the control tower at Chicago's
O'Hare Airport—too many flights waiting to coming in, too
many flights waiting to get out. My own tendency to overbook
my life creates a similar turmoil. This keeps me from focusing
on the things I do best. It eats away time from my healthiest
relationships, for these closest friends are reluctant to put
impossible demands on me. And overbooking saps my strength
and vitality, weakening me and making me vulnerable to disease,
depression, and sin.

Without a strong resolve to say no to most things, I will
never be able to accomplish what I've been called to do.

How does a busy woman say no to more exciting opportunities in order to say yes to God's calling on her life to teach five-year-olds in Sunday school? How does an accountant say no to her manager's suggestion that she get "creative" in balancing the books? How does a brilliant high school student say no to the desire to be involved in everything when confronted with a dozen interesting extracurricular activities that will sap her time and energy, eventually affecting her grades?

In examining the habits and attitudes of those who finish well, I observed that they had somehow learned to override the tendency to overcommit. Doing less has allowed them to do well at what they were called to do.

No Is Always an Option

"We really don't have a choice," he told me. "If I don't take this promotion, I'll never have another opportunity with this company again."

I was talking with a couple whom we had grown to love deeply. He had been asked to move to Detroit to open a new branch of his company. It was a great professional opportunity, but the consequences for his family were devastating. His teenage children and his wife were particularly upset, and she had initiated our meeting.

"You *do* have a choice," I reasoned. "You can *always* say no, and it's important to remember that." I agreed with him that sometimes the consequences of saying no are high. It might cost him a promotion, even a job. But it was an option. Then I asked him to consider the costs of not learning to say no.

"In this situation you will give up a home you love in a community you love. You will give up a church that is having a significant effect on you and your children. You will give up friends you have invested in and who have invested in you.

"I'm really not trying to influence you here (which wasn't entirely true). I just want you to see that the costs of saying yes may be higher than the costs of saying no."

"But I just can't short-circuit my career at this point."

"Have you explored the possibility that there may be other jobs at other companies in your career field located right here? Wouldn't there be other opportunities at those other companies?"

He grudgingly agreed that there might be other options, but his sense of loyalty to his brand and the hope of attaining success within that company appeared to outweigh the personal sacrifices, particularly for his family.

I could see his mind was made up, so I had to back off even though I was concerned for his family. But I was particularly troubled by his insistence that no was not an option. I've heard others verbalize that troubling perspective, and I've seen the pain people go through when they grow to believe this fallacy.

Jesus taught us to consider the cost before making a decision (Matt. 8:18–20). Sometimes though, we don't consider the cost from both perspectives.

Do I Have the Time?

Saying yes to one thing means I must be willing to say no to something else. Time is like money. It must be budgeted, since none of us have an unlimited budget of time. We must learn to function with twenty-four hours in a day. We get in trouble the same way we get in financial trouble. We borrow from tomorrow's resources to pay off today's debts.

When a person buys something with a credit card, he is committing money he doesn't yet have. But optimism tells him he will have plenty of money later, so he presumes upon the future. When the credit card statement comes in, he is obligated to spend that money he previously committed, even if he needs it for something else.

We can do the same thing when we commit ourselves to events in the distant future.

Several months ago I received an invitation to be the speaker for a large senior adult conference. My first impulse when looking at my calendar and finding no other commitments was to say, "Sure. I can do this." But I've learned always to ask for time to make a decision, even if I'm positive about what I'm going to do. That gives me time to remember that every day is a busy day. While the calendar looked clear six months in advance, the days of this conference would no doubt be busy as well.

I began asking more questions. Could I afford to be gone from the church? A look at my schedule found no obvious conflicts. In fact, two days of the three-day conference were my regularly scheduled days off, so I was free to use them as I chose. Then did I want to give up the chance to rest and spend time with my family that week? What was on Susan's calendar that I didn't know about? Since going would involve overnight travel, I had to take travel time into consideration. I also remembered how tired I am after flying. How would this trip affect me in the days immediately following?

All these questions helped me decide whether I had the time. But that was just the first decision I had to make.

Do I Really Want to Spend It?

If I plan my calendar on a first-come, first-served basis, I can often find myself regretting an earlier commitment to something good because it prevents me from participating in something better. On the other hand, many of life's most rewarding experiences aren't recognizable from a distance.

Were there other motives that needed to be considered? Well, yes. The conference was going to be held at a beautiful hotel on the beach in Destin, Florida, one of the most scenic places in the country. The people extending the invitation also offered to cover my wife's expenses so she could attend with me. Visions of candlelight dinners and boat rides around the harbor began to make the offer even more tempting.

While I had enough details about the opportunity, I still had some questions to ask myself. What were the consequences of declining this invitation? My answers ran the gamut from spiritual to practical to embarrassing. There might be someone in that audience whom God could touch through my personality. I might not get another opportunity to minister to this particular group. The budget is always tight, and the honorarium from this event could come in handy. It makes me feel bad to say no to people who have flattered me by asking for my help.

All of us need a spouse or friend who will hold us accountable, asking us to offer a rational justification for our decision to take on yet another duty. I call my wife, Susan, my "just say no" advocate. She knows my strengths and weaknesses better than I, so I rarely accept anything without consulting her.

I also had to ask, What other possible things could come up that I didn't yet know about? The conference was in May—a month full of end-of-school activities and opportunities to spend time with people I love. What if, by accepting this invitation, I had to turn down an invitation to something I would enjoy even more, or something really important to our kids?

Another question I must ask is, Is this something that fits who I am and who God has gifted me to be? This isn't always the first question I ask, but it should be. Finding your calling has been an underlying theme throughout this book. Without this, we waste time and energy on lesser things.

As I prayed, I made a list of reasons to go and reasons to decline. Here is my list of reasons to go:
- Teaching is my primary spiritual gift; this is an invitation to teach God's Word.
- A chance to enjoy a beautiful location with my wife.
- A chance to work again with a worship leader whom I enjoy.
- A chance to enjoy a beautiful location with my wife (the fact that it kept coming up was a clue).

And here is my list of reasons to decline:
- This isn't my target audience.

That was it. One point. At this point in my life, most of my speaking time is dedicated to helping people in ministry. When I teach pastors and church leaders, my time has a greater potential impact for God's kingdom. The research needed to prepare to teach seminars and workshops for pastors usually benefits my ministry at my own church. This event did not fit any of those criteria, and there were many speakers who specialize in senior adult ministry who could do a better job than I could.

When I weighed the evidence, I finally concluded that I needed to pass on this opportunity. But I was reluctant to call the person back and say, "Thanks, but I cannot help you this time." Why is it so hard just to say no?

That Tough Little Two-Letter Word

It's hard to suppress the temptation to say yes. When we say yes, we can make someone else happy, and most of us have an unhealthy need for the approval of others. We sometimes agree to take on one more project at work because we have unrealistic expectations about our capacity for productivity. Until we find ourselves gasping for breath and crushed beneath the load, we think, *I can do this.*

Leaders have learned to ask a busy person if they need something done. They quickly identify people who have the energy, drive, and ability to take on additional responsibility. So to be asked to take additional responsibility affirms our ego. It says, "I'm needed and important." That in itself is a powerful motivator to accept any and all opportunities. Along with that, the kind of person who gets opportunities is the kind of person who is always looking for new challenges.

There are also some darker motives that make it hard to say no. One is a feeling of guilt, either self-produced or provided by the person asking for our help. "If you don't teach four-year-olds in Sunday school this year, those poor little children will have no one to tell them about Jesus."

Sometimes we agree to something we really can't juggle because we have a high need to control every situation. Our skewed thinking tells us, "I'm the only one who could possibly do this right."

Some of us feel the need to stay perpetually busy, either to mask our pain or to gain a sense of self-worth. Getting at the root of this destructive habit will pay big dividends in emotional health and spiritual well-being.

"I'm Sorry I Won't Be Able to Help You This Time"

Part of our fear of saying no is trying to articulate our decision to others. More often than not, there is no one single reason why we must decline. In many situations we would be better off to offer our regrets and move on rather than trying to explain.

Sometimes we don't want another responsibility at work because of an already-full plate. Sitting down with our supervisor and presenting our current workload helps shift the responsibility for the decision back to him or her. Maybe some of our work can be reassigned to someone else. Maybe some deadlines can be rearranged. If you really want the new project, you can indicate your interest by suggesting these options. In any event, your supervisor will gain a new appreciation for the work you are doing and might just say, "I need your energy on these more important issues. I'll put someone else on this new project."

Saying No to Myself

Sometimes I want to say no and can't. Everyone seems to have a plan for my life, so I occasionally give in to those expectations.

Sometimes I need to say no and won't. In chapter 2, I talked about how helpful it is to schedule frequent meetings with myself to review my calendar, relationships, and energy level. In addition to daily planning, thirty minutes to an hour each Sunday night helps me review the week behind, plan the week ahead, and consider my effectiveness in my ministry, my

family, and my other interests. I have a few questions in the
front of my journal that I ask myself often:

- Saying yes to God's best means saying no to a host of
  other worthy, exciting, and attractive opportunities. Which
  is this—God's best, or just another good opportunity?
- Have my ambitions become my shackles?
- Am I neglecting my gifts in order to satisfy my
  insecurities?

This meeting with myself gives me better perspective that
anything else I do.

Then I've had to come to terms with some fantasies in my
life. I've always admired Renaissance men like Leonardo
DaVinci. At times I've believed I could achieve high proficiency
in many areas of my life. When I jump into a new hobby or
interest, I need all the tools and toys, all the books and seminars.
I can pick up most things quickly. But once I get into it, I usually begin to lose interest. This means I'm not really cut out to
be a Renaissance man.

We encourage our daughters to try a lot of different activities, but we hope each will find something—music, a sport, a
special interest or hobby—that she can specialize in and thereby
experience the joy of being good at something.

While I enjoy having a broad range of knowledge, I believe
I will have a greater impact with my life if I can focus my energy.
Becoming truly good at anything requires saying no to other
demands on your time and energy.

I've also become increasingly aware of our tendency to seek
joy and satisfaction from what we do or what we are instead of
in *whose we are.*

In his classic book *Desiring God*, John Piper writes:

> The older I get, the more I am persuaded that
> Nehemiah 8:10 is crucial for living and dying well:
> "The joy of the LORD is your strength." As we grow
> older and our bodies weaken, we must learn from the

Puritan pastor Richard Baxter (who died in 1691) to redouble our efforts to find strength from spiritual joy, not natural supplies. He prayed, "May the Living God, who is the portion and rest of the saints, make these our carnal minds so spiritual, and our earthly hearts so heavenly, that loving him, and delighting in him, may be the work of our lives. When delighting in God is the work of our lives (which I call Christian Hedonism), there will be an inner strength for ministries of love to the very end."[16]

In the long run, saying yes to God's desire to be in an intimate relationship with me will satisfy every yearning of my heart. And that makes saying no to secondary things a lot easier.

CHAPTER FIFTEEN

Winners Invest in People

I don't know what the secret of success is, but I do know the secret of failures—trying to please everybody.
—Comedian Bill Cosby

IN 1983 I WAS A YOUNG SERGEANT in the United States Air Force. The woman I rented from came by one day with a proposal. An elderly friend of hers was ill with cancer and needed someone to care for her yard. Would I be interested? If so, my landlady would lower my rent in exchange for yard work for her friend. I agreed to do so, never expecting that life-changing relationships were about to be initiated.

Like too many young people who grow up in church, I had become a prodigal son, cut loose from the anchor of my faith. The congregations during my developmental years had been sources of pain, dysfunctional, and disappointing.

Although I still believed in God and knew I belonged to Christ, I had no need for the church—at least the church as I knew it. Consequently, it wasn't too long before I had developed some habits and a lifestyle that dishonored God. That was about to change.

Dorothy Saults was a strong woman, bold and sassy even as breast cancer revisited her for the second time in her eighth decade of life. She thanked me for agreeing to take care of her yard, but she made it clear that she had a high standard for its appearance.

My visits became weekly during the summer. I would mow the yard and trim around the sidewalks and flower beds. Dorothy would meet me with a cold drink and point out every place where I had been less than perfect. Over time, we began to tell each other our stories.

Seeing People as They Could Be

Our friendship grew closer as Dorothy's illness grew worse. I began to come over frequently to check on her, even as winter came and the yard went to sleep. I soon became a regular for dinner. Ladies from her church kept her supplied with more food than she had appetite for. We would eat together, and she would tell me about her late husband, her children and grandchildren, her life. I would tell her pieces of my background, and over time we began to talk about issues of substance, including our faith. She knew I was living a less-than-godly life, and she gently challenged me about it.

Dorothy also loved to tease me, saying the neighbors were talking about that widow down the street who always had a young single man around the house and that if a scandal broke out it would ruin her reputation. Occasionally, she asked me to drive her ninety miles to the university hospital where she received chemotherapy. That meant I would have to stop the car on the way home and hold her head while she threw up.

One day that spring a round little bald man showed up while I was finishing the yard work. He introduced himself as Tom, a friend of Dorothy's. He was funny and a great storyteller. He invited me out to his farm to see his menagerie of animals.

After that, he seemed to be at Dorothy's house every time I was. It wasn't until I discovered that Tom Bray was her pastor that it dawned on me there was a conspiracy in progress. But by that time, I enjoyed their company so much that I was willing to forgive them.

Although Tom sometimes invited me to church, I knew our friendship was not based on my saying yes. So I welcomed his encouragement but steadfastly refused his invitation.

One Saturday afternoon, Tom came by to tell me that Dorothy had been admitted to the hospital. He stayed just a few minutes. As he was leaving, he asked, "Ed, you seem like a smart guy in a lot of ways. So you must have a plan. What will you have to show for your life when you stand before God? I was just wondering."

His question angered me, and I gave him a rude response. But that question haunted me. Dorothy's illness and poor prognosis had me thinking about death—and life. After a sleepless night, Sunday morning found me seated near the front in Tom's church. By the end of the service, the prodigal son had returned home.

We lost Dorothy the next summer. I had finished my military tour of duty and was back home in New Mexico, unable to attend her funeral. Her daughter called with the news. We wept together. Then she told me how much her mother talked about me and how much she had loved me. "Mom had an eye for special people," she told me. "Now be sure you make something of yourself to prove her right."

Tom's influence in my life has continued to this day. He was the one who helped me select a college, William Jewell—the same one he and his children had attended. He gave a prayer of blessing at our wedding. When I was struggling to come to terms with God's calling on my life for ministry, it was Tom whom I went to for counsel. It was in his church that I preached my first real sermon. I hadn't known him long before I discovered that he had made a similar impact on the lives of dozens of other young servicemen throughout the years, including many who are now in ministry.

Through the years, he's continued to be a mentor and a role model. Although a stroke and other health issues have forced his retirement and limited his mobility, Tom still keeps up with me and prays for me and many other "sons in the ministry."

The last time we were together, I wanted to ask him, "Why did you make time for me? Of all the people around you, why did you invest in me?" But the right opportunity never came.

But I know what his reply would be because I've heard him say it to others. "Because I could see beyond who you were. I could see you were a man whom God could use."

A Hopeful Name

Andrew was the first of John's sons who met Jesus. He then wanted his brother to meet the one who would save the world. We find the account in John 1:42: "And [Andrew] brought [his brother] to Jesus. Jesus looked at him and said, 'You are Simon son of John. You will be called Cephas' (which, when translated, is Peter)."

The name Cephas was Aramaic; Peter was the Greek word for "rock." The name brings to mind such words as *solid, dependable, foundational.* At the time he received his new name, Peter the Rock was anything but. Just a casual look through Scripture reveals he was impulsive, brash, and unpredictable in those days. But look who he became—the preacher whose first sermon resulted in three thousand people coming to saving knowledge of Christ (Acts 2:14–41). Apart from Paul, Peter was the most influential leader of the early church.

Jesus saw Peter as he could be, not as he was.

Some people have the vision and means to build buildings of immense size and commanding attention. Others have the shrewdness to build corporations of great financial strength. When we witness the feats of a Donald Trump or a Bill Gates, we marvel at their drive and ambition. But an even greater respect is due those people who follow Jesus' example and look beyond the obvious. People like Dorothy Saults and Tom Bray are building a legacy of people who are achieving more than they ever dreamed because they could see possibilities in others before they became reality.

Why Make the Time?

Why would a busy person take the time to invest in someone else when that time and energy might be spent instead on their own dreams? Two reasons. First, when you examine the lives of people who invest in others, you almost always discover a chain reaction. They invest in others because someone invested in them. Duplicating the kindness shown them is the only way to repay such a debt of love.

Second, a discerning person will note that the only investment we can make that will have value in heaven is the investment we make in people for the sake of God's kingdom.

Discovering Hidden Talent

When we encounter someone who believes in us when we don't yet believe in ourselves, it changes us forever. I have learned to see myself in a new light after receiving that kind of love and faith. How could I not make a personal priority of developing other people?

How do you know who has the potential to be a rock, even if she acts like a flake right now? What does latent talent look like? How does dormant possibility reveal itself?

On one hand, we can be confident that every person we meet has more capacity for ability than we can see. In theory, investing in anyone could pay big dividends. But not everyone we invest in will blossom or even wants to blossom.

How do we become God's talent scout, learning to see others as he sees them? We begin by praying for God's insight and perspective. If we are serious about being his catalyst in the lives of others, he will give us an intuitive eye. And we must also acknowledge that no investment has a 100-percent guarantee of success. Even though this involves risk, we can begin by looking at the following:

People who work hard. In the 1980s the Tanzanian marathon runner Juma Ikangaa completed more marathons under 2:10

than any runner in history. His secret was his motto: "The will to win means nothing without the will to prepare."[17]

Ikangaa was known for a brutal training schedule, sometimes running over two hundred miles in a single week. The coach who first spotted this farmer's son saw not only potential but also a strong work ethic. One without the other won't yield the same results.

People with whom we have credibility. Influencing another person to pursue a life devoted to fulfilling God's plan for his or her life begins with a relationship. It is usually only after that relationship develops that opportunities for mentoring develop. If you want to build a legacy, seek first to influence the people who are already around you.

People who are willing to dream. Not everyone has the capacity to see beyond the here-and-now. Once trust has been established, conversations of the heart will reveal whether people have allowed themselves to imagine a life of purpose and accomplishment.

People who have influence. In the Book of Acts, we find great examples of how Paul selected people to extend God's ministry. Because he invested his life in Barnabas, Timothy, John Mark, Luke, Lydia, Priscilla and Aquila, and many others, Paul's ministry exploded. All were people of influence, or they had the potential for influence. But not everyone he set his sights on responded. In Acts 26 Paul had the opportunity to confront King Agrippa with the gospel.

> Then Agrippa said to Paul, "Do you think that in such a short time you can persuade me to be a Christian?"
>
> Paul replied, "Short time or long—I pray God that not only you but all who are listening to me today may become what I am, except for these chains" (Acts 26:28–29).

Although Agrippa chose to reject Christ, Paul saw the potential within him to influence the world should he choose to receive Christ. That willingness to risk is a characteristic worth emulating.

People who value character as well as accomplishment. Raw ambition will take a person far—at least far in pursuing his or her own vision. A person who will pursue God's preferred vision for his life must withstand the temptations of power, position, wealth, and self-glorification if they are to finish well. That's why mentors must model a servant heart and the spirit of Christ.

People who can work on a team. Jenny Thompson is the most decorated Olympic woman in America. With ten Olympic medals in swimming in the last three Olympics, she also has won more medals in swimming than any other Olympic athlete of any nation. Eight of those ten medals were gold.

However, this twenty-seven-year-old swimmer from Dove, New Hampshire, didn't win a single gold medal in individual events; she won them in relay races, a team event, with three other swimmers.

As a result, some people have questioned whether Jenny's swimming accomplishments ought to rank her with the "great" Olympic champions.

I find Jenny's accomplishments refreshing in the ego-driven American culture. With so many athletes seeing their own fame and fortune, Jenny is a great example of a person whose genuine success came as a team player.

The Cost of Mentoring

We must scrutinize our motives to determine why we are ready to invest in another. Are we looking for someone to pump up our own ego? Are we desiring to build our own kingdom on the backs of others? Or are we genuinely interested in building God's kingdom by seeking and developing others?

In Matthew's Gospel, the mother of two of Jesus' disciples came to him, asking him to grant her sons positions of honor. Jesus discerned that her motive (and that of her sons, who most likely put her up to it) was not one that would allow them to withstand the hardship of what loomed ahead. He then used the occasion to remind the other disciples about the self-sacrificing spirit they would need to build his kingdom.

"When the ten heard about this, they were indignant with the two brothers. Jesus called them together and said, 'You know that the rulers of the Gentiles lord it over them, and their high officials exercise authority over them. Not so with you. Instead, whoever wants to become great among you must be your servant, and whoever wants to be first must be your slave— just as the Son of Man did not come to be served, but to serve, and to give his life as a ransom for many'" (Matt. 20:24–28).

Following Jesus' Example

As was always the case, Jesus backed his words with his example. His willingness to wash the disciples' feet showed them and us that his love compels us to serve one another: "I have set you an example that you should do as I have done for you. I tell you the truth, no servant is greater than his master, nor is a messenger greater than the one who sent him. Now that you know these things, you will be blessed if you do them" (John 13:15–17).

Paul expounded upon this theme of leading by serving in Philippians 2, perhaps the most descriptive passage in Scripture about the nature of Jesus Christ, why he came to redeem us and the implications for all who call him Lord. Paul reminds us:

Your attitude should be the same as that of Christ Jesus:

> Who, being in very nature God,
> did not consider equality with God something to be
> grasped,
> but made himself nothing,
> taking the very nature of a servant,
> being made in human likeness.
> And being found in appearance as a man,
> he humbled himself
> and became obedient to death—
> even death on a cross! (Phil. 2:5–9).

Although *mentoring* is a buzzword in pop culture these days, to invest in someone for the building of God's kingdom is radically different from helping someone feel good about himself or perpetuating one's own success in the marketplace.

Oprah Winfrey recently said, "This is the defining question of my life. How do you use your life to best serve *yourself* and extend it to the world?"[18]

From all accounts it appears that Oprah is doing both. Although her words sound noble and probably reflect the majority view in today's world, the first part of her question differs significantly from God's definition of a life well lived. Jesus said, "But seek ye first *the kingdom of God*, and his righteousness; and all these things shall be added unto you" (Matt. 6:33 KJV, emphasis added).

When we pass along a passion for kingdom priorities, we have made perhaps our greatest investment in the life of another.

CHAPTER SIXTEEN

Winners Keep Learning and Growing

*"Give me wisdom and knowledge, that I may lead this people, for
who is able to govern this great people of yours?"*
—King Solomon's prayer, 2 Chronicles 1:10

A COLLEGE CERAMICS TEACHER ANNOUNCED on the first day of
class that he would give his students two options for making an
A in his course. Option one would be based on the *quantity* of
work they produced. The professor would bring in a bathroom
scale on the final day of class and weigh each student's work—
fifty pounds of pots would be an A, forty pounds a B, and so on.
Option two was to be graded on the *quality* of their work. The
student need only produce one pot all semester, but it must be
perfect.

A curious thing happened when the semester ended. The
best quality pots in class were in the piles of those who had gone
for the quantity grade. It seems that while the "quantity" group
was busy churning out the pots and getting hands-on experience, the "quality" group had sat around theorizing about perfection, then had little to show for their efforts except
extravagant theories and a pile of dead clay.

This parable speaks to me about the power of learning by
doing. We are all faced with the choice of either modifying our
dreams or magnifying our skills. Skills are enhanced by doing—
not reading or studying—something. And the better you
become at your key skills, the more you accomplish in less time.

We are living in a complex world with a global economy. We
are constantly bombarded by new information, new insights,

and new technologies. We are kept off balance by previously unheard-of avenues for business, a staggering array of high-tech tools, and an ever-changing worldview. Add to this the reality that few companies fail to give their people any sense of job security, and all of us have to stay sharp in our job-hunting and interviewing skills.

Those who don't keep up get left behind in the dust. Or run over.

In many fields it is not just technical knowledge that changes. Basic philosophies and principles of doing business no longer apply. Who can really explain the recent phenomenon of Internet companies, so-called dot-coms, which have yet to turn a profit but made hundreds of millions of dollars by going public? It defies every economic principle prior to this generation.

The only way to stay ahead of rapid change is to commit to lifelong learning and growing. Formal education is only the beginning for those who want to finish well in life. We must consider every day of our lives to be a day in the classroom of life.

As much as we would like to think this is something new for our generation, Scripture provides us with examples of others who practiced this principle.

Moses was one of the best-trained leaders in the ancient world. As the adopted son of Pharaoh's daughter, he received the finest education of the day. No doubt schooled in mathematics, languages, and Egyptian history, he was also being groomed for a major role in the government or military. Strategies and theories and philosophies of warfare and leadership were drilled into him. Opportunities for leadership were offered him at an early age.

And yet when he began the leadership role for which he had been born, one of his greatest lessons came not from the

Egyptian university but from his father-in-law Jethro, the sheepherder.

We find the story in Exodus 18:9–24. After his encounter with the burning bush, Moses went back to Egypt, leaving his wife and children with her family. By the time they reunited, many incredible things had happened. You can picture them sitting around the campfire in the evenings as Moses tried to tell them all that God had done. Jethro was particularly impressed by God's hand.

Jethro said, "'Praise be to the LORD, who rescued you from the hand of the Egyptians and of Pharaoh, and who rescued the people from the hand of the Egyptians. Now I know that the LORD is greater than all other gods, for he did this to those who had treated Israel arrogantly.'

"Then Jethro, Moses' father-in-law, brought a burnt offering and other sacrifices to God, and Aaron came with all the elders of Israel to eat bread with Moses' father-in-law in the presence of God" (Exod. 18:10–12).

But the old shepherd was not so impressed with his son-in-law's leadership skills. Moses and his brother Aaron had been the primary leaders of this huge crowd of people. God had given the law to Moses on Mount Sinai; therefore, he assumed responsibility to enforce and interpret that law for the people. The Bible tells it this way:

> The next day Moses took his seat to serve as judge for the people, and they stood around him from morning till evening. When his father-in-law saw all that Moses was doing for the people, he said, "What is this you are doing for the people? Why do you alone sit as judge, while all these people stand around you from morning till evening?"
>
> Moses answered him, "Because the people come to me to seek God's will. Whenever they have a dispute, it is brought to me, and I decide between the parties and inform them of God's decrees and laws."

Moses' father-in-law replied, "What you are doing is not good. You and these people who come to you will only wear yourselves out. The work is too heavy for you; you cannot handle it alone. Listen now to me and I will give you some advice, and may God be with you. You must be the people's representative before God and bring their disputes to him. Teach them the decrees and laws, and show them the way to live and the duties they are to perform. But select capable men from all the people—men who fear God, trustworthy men who hate dishonest gain—and appoint them as officials over thousands, hundreds, fifties and tens. Have them serve as judges for the people at all times, but have them bring every difficult case to you; the simple cases they can decide themselves. That will make your load lighter, because they will share it with you. If you do this and God so commands, you will be able to stand the strain, and all these people will go home satisfied." Moses listened to his father-in-law and did everything he said (Exod. 18:13–24).

Jethro had never led an army, never sat in a governmental post, never received any formal management training. Yet Moses, through God's help, had just liberated over two million slaves and led them toward freedom; Moses, the best educated, most thoroughly trained man of his day, listened to the advice of this simple but wise man who had herded goats and sheep with his isolated clan in the Sinai Peninsula all his life.

Moses had lived with Jethro's clan for forty years. He had grown to know and appreciate Jethro's wisdom and insight. He was willing to listen to good advice, no matter who was the source.

All of us who want to finish well in life will apply this principle to life.

A while back another pastor took me to lunch to talk about preaching. I recommended a book I had just read on effective public speaking, *Simply Speaking*, written by Peggy Noonan, former speechwriter for Ronald Reagan.

"What could I possibly learn from a woman speech writer?" he asked. *Probably nothing*, I thought to myself, set back by his arrogance.

Starting Point

Solomon began his quest for knowledge and wisdom with prayer. Martin Luther wrote, "I have often learned more in one prayer than I have been able to glean from much reading and reflection." Lifelong learning both begins and ends with the origin of truth. Regardless of your field of interest, God already knows all there is to know about it. Make sure you seek him first, early, and often in your search for understanding. Not only will he reveal to you the timeless truths of Scripture, but he will also guide your awareness to what is going on around you.

Is lifelong learning, then, simply a matter of paying attention every day to nuggets of wisdom from anyone and everyone? Partly. But we can also be proactive in developing our lifelong learning plans. My continuing education comes primarily from books I read and conferences I attend.

Reading on Purpose

It's no secret that I'm a bookaholic. I should be in a twelve-step group. I have to sneak books into my house. My ministry budget for books is always tapped by midyear. Not a week goes by that I don't hear of a book I *need* to read. I read for fun, but more importantly, I read to stay on top of the expanding skills necessary for my profession. Here are some things I've learned about reading for knowledge.

Learning to scan a book. This is an art well worth developing. By reading the flyleaf and the table of contents, I can usually tell if a book is worth buying. Access to Internet bookstores allows me to do searches on a particular topic and read a synopsis online. Here are some questions I ask myself while browsing. *Is this book merely describing a problem, or does it offer solutions?* Discerning a problem with the status quo is no great art, in my view. I'm looking for help from people who have some solutions to offer.

Is the author prescribing timeless principles that can be transferred from one application to another, or is he advocating methods that are trendy and nontransferable? Management theories, for example, change frequently. (In recent years we've been asked to buy into management by objective, management by walking around, total quality management, etc.) More helpful to me are books that offer leadership principles that never change. I can then contextualize them to my situation.

Is this author a doer or a talker? Surprisingly, not all authors who speak with great authority actually have experience. Sometimes they just have theories about "what ought to work." I learn best from people who have actually field-tested their theories.

I've also learned that I don't have to finish a book in order for it to impact my life in a positive way. I recently devoted myself to study change and the leader's role as a change agent. I picked up about six books on the subject that met the above criteria. I got more useful information from the first three chapters of one than I got from all the others. But I never finished it. I know where it is if I ever want to go back to the subject, though.

Preserve Your Study

I write in my books, underlining insightful passages and making notes in the margins and on blank pages. For a recent Bible study I taught on marriage, I referenced a book I first read about fifteen years ago. On the inside front cover I found the note I was looking for. "How to recover from an affair, page 65." I immediately had my information.

I file my books topically—leadership, theology, change, worship, etc. I don't tend to remember exact titles or even authors' names, but I can almost always find a book if it is filed with other books of like subject matter. Your system for retrieving information may vary, but I encourage you to devise a way to take notes on what you read for later use. Several software packages exist that promise great things. While it is really difficult to catalog a library once you have several thousand volumes, I'm making the effort in order to better use the resources God has given me.

Specialize for a Period of Time

For years, I read everything I could get my hands on regarding communication and leadership. Those two subjects address the most challenging issues for those in ministry, and they also promise the most reward when learned and applied. But eventually for all of us, there comes a point where your knowledge outruns your ability to apply the information you've learned. By no means do I know all there is to know about leadership or communication. But because I've read so widely, I find many new books on the subject are simply rewriting the same basic information I've already received elsewhere. I still scan all the new books, though, hoping for that occasional breakthrough work.

In 1999, for example, I devoted most of my study to the subject of worship. I read and reread everything of substance in print on the subject. I participate on our church's worship planning team, which includes music, drama, and other visual arts, as well as the technical capabilities that make it all possible.

I want to make sure I lead from a growing theological and philosophical position, not from one of musical preference or tradition. As a pastor, not a musician, I may be lacking in musical ability, but no one on our team will have a better understanding of the history and biblical perspective of worship.

Practical Skills

All of us occasionally have to invest time in learning how to use the tools that are so much a part of our lives. Those who have yet to make the computer a part of their toolbox are intimidated, believing that the learning curve is too steep. In reality, most people can learn to use E-mail and do basic word processing after completing a one-day seminar.

I have felt the freedom to learn how to work a computer without worrying about how a computer works. I liken this to the millions of people who know how to drive a car but don't even know how to open the hood. Most areas have good community colleges that offer practical instruction in skills that help us work more efficiently without going into a lot of technical detail.

I am seeing many retired adults who no longer need computer skills for their jobs take such classes in order to E-mail distant children and grandchildren, missionaries, and old classmates or friends from military service.

Once the initial intimidation of technology is overcome, it's time to get some specialized training. I would hate to go back to sermon preparation without Internet access. But learning how to maximize search engines and narrow my searches took some time to learn. E-mail allows me to keep in touch with far more people than phones or letters ever could. Then, learning skills like how to E-mail to groups in my address book has really given me a boost in effectiveness in communication.

Seminars and one-day workshops have been good investments for me. Aside from the specific topic being taught at such conferences, they give me an opportunity to build my network of like-minded people. In recent years I have tried to attend such conferences with someone I work with so that we can process what we've learned together.

Formal degrees are becoming possible even for those who thought they would never have the opportunity. Many colleges and universities have both graduate and undergraduate degree programs with curriculum and scheduling designed for busy working adults.

I've discovered that a great way to learn new information is to become obligated to teach it. I speak at several conferences each year—some for writers, some for pastors. I recently spoke at a preaching conference in Mississippi where I had been assigned two topics on which I had never spoken. I accepted the assignment because I was interested in the subject matter, and I knew the responsibility of teaching the material would ensure that I had a firm grasp of the material.

Although the turnout for the conference was lighter than those planning it had expected, from my perspective it was a success. I had grown in the process and was able to put into practice the very next Sunday the material I had learned in order to teach.

Immersion Learning

When staffs of international corporations need language training, they often choose a school that follows the "immersion" philosophy. By learning, say, Spanish, in a Spanish-speaking country, they are literally forced to exercise their fledging language skills at every turn—at the market or the dinner table, on television and radio, nothing but Spanish. The ear picks up nuances of dialect and pronunciation. Verb tenses suddenly become important.

It's like the old joke preachers tell. A young pastor called his former seminary professor late at night. "Prof, you've got to help me. The head deacon in my church just died, and I've got to officiate at his funeral tomorrow."

The professor was a bit irritated. "You know we covered that in class."

"I know," said the desperate pastor. "But this guy's really dead!"

There's nothing like a crisis to create a desire to learn.

If you have lost a passion for learning somewhere along the line, here are two suggestions. First, immerse yourself in something new that frightens you. Jump into a situation in which you are forced to learn. Experience the discomfort, even terror, of not knowing something you need to know. Then discover the motivation and ability to concentrate that comes with that discomfort, together with the confidence gained from facing your fears. A friend who has a fear of heights told me recently about the absolute terror he faced on a high-ropes course, followed immediately by the rush of accomplishment that came from doing something he dreaded.

Second, make learning and growing fun again. Take up a new hobby with a friend, someone who knows how to make you laugh. Set up some fun rewards for yourself when you finish that course, read that book, or attain that certification.

If you view the pursuit of knowledge as an annoyance or an unfortunate necessity, learning becomes virtually impossible. But when it becomes both a challenge and a game, you'll be amazed at how quickly you pick up new skills and how well you retain them.

CHAPTER SEVENTEEN

Winners Know When to Pull the Trigger

As the time approached for him to be taken up to heaven,
Jesus resolutely set out for Jerusalem.
—Luke 9:51

MAKING A DECISION—any decision—can be tough for some people. When that decision must be made in the midst of stress, fatigue, or emotional upheaval, it becomes even more difficult.

Ever come home late from work to a tired family who has also made one-too-many decisions? In the chaos of the day, dinner plans fell by the wayside, so someone suggests going out to eat.

"Where do you want to eat?" Dad will ask.

"McDonald's!" shouts the six-year-old. "We want McDonald's!"

"It doesn't matter to me," replies Mom, ignoring the growing chorus. "What sounds good to you?"

"McDonald's!" yells the other kid. "We want McDonald's!"

"How about Peking Palace?"

"No, I thought it had really gone downhill last time we ate there."

By now, both kids are jumping up and down. "McDonald's! McDonald's!"

"I vote for any place that doesn't have golden arches on the napkins."

"Hey, I know. Let's try that new place on Moores Lane. The Cooker, I think it's called."

"Not tonight. I've heard it's kind of pricey and the wait is terrible." As the war chant for Happy Meals grows to a crescendo, the tired father caves in. "Look, I don't really care, and these kids get out of control when they're hungry. Let's just take them to McDonald's and be done with it."

Cheers go up for Dad. Mom lacks the strength to counter, so off they go. The parents stand at the counter waiting for service, wondering why they are there again when there are so many other choices in restaurants.

A decision was made. By someone. But the people who will pay for the decision are the most dissatisfied with what was decided.

The above scenario is, of course, purely fictional, and it bears no semblance to any family living at my house. Admittedly, its impact is minimal. The inability to make a decision about where to eat ranks low on the list of things that determine the outcome of your life.

But we've all allowed decisions to be made for us when we lacked the interest, courage, creativity, or energy to make them. Some of those decisions we make, or allow others to make for us, have significant consequences.

Decisions about our education, where we'll live, how we'll earn a living, whom we'll marry or not marry, whether to have children, whether to give more than lip service to Christ—all these decisions are ours to make. I hear too many people express regret over decisions they failed to make, or which others made for them.

"I became a teacher because my mother told me it was a good job for a woman."

"After I married Karen, she convinced me I was wasting my time to pursue my music. I believed her and have been miserable ever since."

"I decided not to go to college because I didn't have a clear idea what I wanted to study. Now I realize that a big reason for attending college is to have a bigger world exposed to you."

What we're talking about can be called by many names. Failure to pull the trigger may be the result of procrastination, indecision, hesitation, or fear of commitment. Sometimes we won't pull the trigger when we can't see the target clearly. That is a matter of *vision*. Other times, it is because we really don't want to shoot the target in our sights. That is a matter of *passion*. We may fail to act because we lack confidence or a sense of certainty.

Andy Stanley, pastor of Northpoint Community Church in Alpharetta, Georgia, taught in detail on this subject at the Catalyst Leadership Conference. He said: "Uncertainty is not an indication of poor leadership. Rather it indicates a need for leadership. The nature of leadership demands that there always be an element of uncertainty. The temptation is to think, 'If I were a good leader, I would know exactly what to do.' Increased responsibility means dealing more with more intangibles and therefore more complex uncertainty. Leaders can afford to be uncertain, but we cannot afford to be unclear. People will not follow fuzzy leadership."[19]

A general leading troops into battle may be uncertain about the outcome. But he must lead with certainty, engaging the enemy by using the best plan he can imagine.

What do most of us do when we are uncertain? We fail to act, paralyzed by our indecision. What we don't know is that putting off a decision really is a decision—a decision to postpone something that may or may not need to be postponed.

First Things First

Making good decisions is a matter of having good counsel. God's Spirit is known as the Counselor. God has no reason to keep his will for our lives a secret. As long as we are this side of heaven, we may struggle with inner conflict between our desires and his desires. But knowing when to pull the trigger becomes a much easier decision when we are submitting ourselves daily to God and his plan for our lives.

John 15:7 is a familiar verse to many: "If you remain in me and my words remain in you, ask whatever you wish, and it will be given you." We often think of it in terms of material needs. However, if we are committed to remaining in communion with Christ and are willing to obey once his will is revealed, he will guide us in every decision.

Reading the Signs

Having the confidence to pull the trigger when it is time depends on being able to read the signs or clues around us.

When I was working as a hunting guide many years ago, one of our toughest tasks was reading the signs to know if the game we were pursuing was in the immediate area. Tracks, droppings, bedding areas, and young trees trashed by antlers were signs that elk were in the vicinity. It's pointless to hunt for elk in areas where there are no elk.

Some people have the uncanny ability to read the signs around them. Some have a sixth sense about when to invest heavily in the stock market and when to pull out and lay low for a while. Others have the ability to spot a product that will catch on, and they get in on the first wave of a marketing trend. To the outsider, it appears they have some sixth sense. In reality, whether they can articulate it or not, these people have the capacity to decipher clues in their environment.

Sir Arthur Conan Doyle, creator of the fictional detective Sherlock Holmes, reportedly told of a time when he climbed into a taxicab in Paris. Before he could utter a word, the driver turned to him and asked, "Where can I take you, Mr. Doyle?"

Doyle was flabbergasted. He asked the driver if he had ever seen him before.

"No, sir," the driver responded, "I have never seen you before. But this morning's paper had a story about you being on vacation in Marseilles. This is the taxi stand where people who return from Marseilles always come. Your skin color tells me you have been on vacation. The ink-spot on your right index finger suggests to me that you are a writer. Your clothing is very English, not French. Adding up all those pieces of information, I deduced that you are Sir Arthur Conan Doyle."

"This is truly amazing!" the writer exclaimed. "You are a real-life counterpart to my fictional creation, Sherlock Holmes."

"There was one other clue," the driver said.

"What was that?"

"Your name is on the front of your suitcase."

If only all clues were that obvious!

Excuses

There are a variety of personality inventories on the market that describe the two basic approaches to decision making. One approach is rational and thoughtful, with a need to get all the pertinent data in hand before making a decision. The other approach relies more on intuition—how the decision feels. It seems to me that most marriages are laboratories in which these two approaches often bang heads. There is usually a *thinker* and a *feeler* in every marriage.

I need more information. Sometimes that is exactly what we need to make a good decision. When we need a household appliance, for example, I could go in one appliance store known for relatively good prices, look at the models, and then make a decision. I am more of a feeler.

My wife, on the other hand, is likely to look around that store, then go home and check out each brand's strengths and weaknesses on the *Consumer Reports* Web site. Then she will visit a few other stores and compare prices yet again. It may take her weeks to process the information to the point that she is comfortable making a decision. She is a thinker.

It just doesn't "feel" right. This is the excuse of feelers like me. I lean toward impulsiveness, making decisions because of some vague sense in my gut. I trust that gut feeling, but occasionally I will postpone what seems to be a natural decision simply because of an uneasiness I feel.

We can have a tendency to spiritualize this hazy excuse by saying, "I just didn't have a sense of peace about it" or "The Lord just hasn't confirmed it in my spirit." That may be true, but then again, if we're honest, we've made many other decisions without considering their spiritual consequences and never had a qualm.

I find that putting my uneasiness on paper helps me discern if I am sensing something from God or just masking the real reason I'm hesitant behind God-talk.

I need more time to make sure it's right. This excuse is rooted in perfectionism, which almost always manifests the fear of making mistakes. The perfectionist doesn't want to put her name on something that may not be her best work. Artists, writers, and other creative people struggle with this one in particular.

The first book I edited was a collection of sermon illustrations. I was very proud the day I held the finished copy in my hands with my name on the book jacket. I opened the book to a random page. To my horror, my eyes immediately fell to a badly misspelled word. That book had gone through a series of spell checking, both manually, by computer, and at least four pairs of professionally trained eyes. Still the mistake came through.

The next book in the series was full of humorous stories for preaching and teaching. I obsessed about the details of that book and couldn't bear to let it finally go to the publisher. When that book finally came out, the error was even more glaring— the other editor on the project was omitted from the cover. I had not been responsible for that one, but nonetheless I let that mistake bother me for a week.

If we refuse to pull the trigger until we have all the facts and have worked out all the details, we will have few opportunities in life. Seldom does opportunity come without some accompanying risks. When asked about his prolific output, one writer who would prefer to remain unnamed recently quipped, "I'm known more for getting it out quick than getting it out slick."

When . . . (the kids are gone), I'll do it. These kinds of excuses are always suspect. They are based on the notion that there will be a better time to act in the future.

We forget that no stage of life is easier—they are all just different. Suppose a young man really wants to go back to school to get the training necessary to make a career change. Making that kind of change usually results in financial hardship, which may seem devastating when there are preschoolers in the house and their mother stays home to care for them. But those changes won't be any easier when those kids are in college and those tuition bills are rolling in every month. By the time the children are out of college, there is just a short window of opportunity to do some last-minute saving for retirement, and then of course by retirement there's little point in finding a new career.

I tend to operate by the following principle: If I sense God is leading, I consider the timing to be now. If it is not, he'll reveal that to me as I strive to obey. To postpone obedience until it is more convenient for me falls in the category of sin.

The wisest man who ever lived said, "Whatever your hand finds to do, do it with all your might, for in the grave, where you are going, there is neither working nor planning nor knowledge nor wisdom" (Eccles. 9:10).

Weighing Risk

Gaining a better perspective on decision making requires asking a lot of personal questions. What losses and failures are acceptable right now? Which are unacceptable? How can I grow without making mistakes? Whose reputation am I protecting by not acting—mine or God's? What does that say about my source of strength?

We dread a lot of decisions that really have minimal risk. I stood in line the other day for what seemed like an eternity waiting for a woman to decide what kind of ice cream she wanted. After the rest of us in line had grown old and gray, she decided on vanilla. I felt like leading a cheer—"Yea! She finally made a decision!"

In the marketplace the ability to make decisions is often greatly rewarded. Next time you are having problems making a decision, break it down into a series of smaller decisions:

1. What is my real objective here? *Why* must I decide?
2. What is my deadline? *When* must I decide?
3. What *new information* do I need before I decide?
4. Can I break the decision into *smaller parts*?
5. Will this decision be *final*, or can I change my mind later?
6. What *risks* are involved? Are they worth it?
7. What *fears* are keeping me from a decision? Are they real or imagined?

If you agonize over decisions, use these insignificant opportunities to practice making them. Next time you are in line for ice cream, blurt out the first exotic flavor that comes to mind. Chances are you'll enjoy it, and if you don't, at least you'll make everyone in line behind you happier.

Avoiding the Pendulum Swing

Coming to grips with indecision doesn't mean becoming hasty or impulsive. Jesus warned his disciples of the dangers of not first counting the cost before executing a decision.

> Suppose one of you wants to build a tower. Will he not first sit down and estimate the cost to see if he has enough money to complete it? For if he lays the foundation and is not able to finish it, everyone who sees it will ridicule him, saying, "This fellow began to build and was not able to finish."

Or suppose a king is about to go to war against another king. Will he not first sit down and consider whether he is able with ten thousand men to oppose the one coming against him with twenty thousand? If he is not able, he will send a delegation while the other is still a long way off and will ask for terms of peace. In the same way, any of you who does not give up everything he has cannot be my disciple (Luke 14:28–33).

Following Christ, according to Jesus, may cost a person everything he has. Once that decision has been made, we make an amazing discovery. Every other decision we'll ever make becomes easier because we are no longer making decisions by ourselves.

Jesus said, "But when he, the Spirit of truth, comes, he will guide you into all truth. He will not speak on his own; he will speak only what he hears, and he will tell you what is yet to come. He will bring glory to me by taking from what is mine and making it known to you. All that belongs to the Father is mine. That is why I said the Spirit will take from what is mine and make it known to you" (John 16:13–15).

It's easier to pull the trigger when you've got the confidence that God is leading.

CHAPTER EIGHTEEN

Winners Prioritize Relationships

The difference between a successful person and others is not a lack of strength, not a lack of knowledge, but rather a lack of will.
—Football legend Vince Lombardi

ONE OF THE BIGGEST MYTHS OF OUR DAY IS THIS: "You can have it all." While there are a few people in the world with unlimited financial resources, just about everyone I know must learn to live within a fixed income—or pay drastic consequences.

One of the simplest budgeting methods is the so-called envelope system. You make envelopes for each area of spending—Tithe, Groceries, Utilities, and other predictable categories. If you run out of money in your grocery envelope before payday and still need milk or bread, then your only option is to take money from some other envelope.

What few of us clearly understand is that our other, more precious resources have limitations as well. Take time, for example. I have only twenty-four hours to spend today. No more, no less. In an earlier chapter, we looked at the essential habit of learning to say no to demands on our time that distract us from our life's mission. With an hour I can watch television, exercise, coach my daughter's basketball team, or sleep. But I cannot do more than one thing with that hour, at least not very well. So when I spend it on something frivolous, I must rob an hour from some other envelope labeled "ministry," "family," or "sleep" to get the important stuff completed.

Similarly, I only have so much emotional energy to give away. And I only have enough time and energy to invest in a finite number of people. Imagine a stack of envelopes with the names of all the people that I interact with on a regular basis. Who's going to get robbed in order to pick up the overdraft in some other relationship? Because we fail to recognize our emotional limitations, developing an intentional approach to relationships is one of the most difficult habits to comprehend. But without it we are far less likely to make the best choices in our relationships.

Top Ten List: Why We Need an Intentional Approach to Relationships

1. Most of us give away our relational energy on a first-come, first-served basis.
2. None of us have all the relational energy we need for everyone we want to spend time with.
3. We don't always know when we are running out of relational energy.
4. We haven't learned to monitor our relational energy.
5. We'll be filled with remorse if we get to life's end and discover that we've given the best of ourselves to people that weren't that important to us.
6. The demands for my time and attention will always exceed my supply.
7. We end up spending our "personal" time on everyone but ourselves.
8. Being overextended for long periods of time makes us grouchy and susceptible to sin.
9. We grow cynical, believing *everyone* wants something from us.
10. We won't have the time or energy to face new challenges and seize new opportunities if we allow ourselves to become depleted.

How do I monitor myself to make sure I'm giving my best to those who matter most? It begins by considering my relational assets—what I have to offer others.

Relational Assets

The ability to influence. Parents have incredible potential to influence their children. This elevates the parent-child relationship to the highest order. Baseball star Cal Ripken says the wisest advice he ever received about parenting came not from child development experts but from a former Orioles teammate named Tim Hulett, whom Ripken regards as "the best dad I've ever known."

Ripken recalls a clubhouse conversation when Hulett told him, "Your little ones are a blank tape, constantly running and recording information. Whose information do you want on that tape? Yours or somebody else's?"

Ripkin's ice-blue eyes locked in on Hulett. "I want *my* information on that tape," he declared.[20]

The ability to listen. My daughters have been known to snap their fingers in my face and say, "Earth to Dad. Come in, please." When I come home with my tank dry, I find that paying attention to others is hard work. That's why some people choose to escape into television or the Internet. Electronic appliances don't demand too much from you.

The ability to stay connected in spite of tension. If I have no emotional reserves, I'll tend to jettison relationships that tax me. Not every difficult alliance should be abandoned. Sometimes I need to stay engaged in a tough relationship so God can use that relationship as a rasp to smooth the rough edges of my character.

The ability to encourage and to bless. Nothing builds relationships like genuine affirmation. God often uses those who practice encouragement to generate something miraculous in another person's life.

But I can't share these assets when I'm in a needy state myself. Therefore, I need people investing into my life the same emotional capital that I'm seeking to give others.

Investing My Assets

In my quest for finishing well at life, I'm learning to ask the following questions:

Whom am I spending the best part of my life with? In today's world, it is possible to know hundreds of people. But usually there is a much smaller number that we interact with closely. Family, coworkers, and friends are the most likely givers and recipients of emotional capital.

What influence are they having on me? Try identifying those people who may be having a mostly negative influence first. (Some names come to mind immediately.) Then list those with a positive influence.

What influence am I having on them? Again, two lists will emerge—those for whom our relationship is beneficial and those who find me a drain on their lives.

Here's an easy exercise that helps illustrate this. Draw a picture of a big holding tank. Pretend it stores your emotional assets. Next, draw a bunch of little pipes around the bottom that are draining the tank, and a bunch of little pipes coming in the top that are filling the tank.

Now, begin to fill in names on each set of pipes. Don't be surprised if some names appear on both. If you'll invest a little time right now in this exercise, you'll begin to have a pretty good idea about how you can be more proactive in your relationships.

Draining Relationships

Anyone who needs something from me falls into this category. Our spouses and children, employers and employees, customers and vendors can all be demanding at times, even if the relationship is a healthy one. We cannot delete all draining relationships from our lives, nor should we. Part of our reason for living is to serve others. The Bible tells us that "even the Son of Man did not come to be served, but to serve, and to give his life as a ransom for many" (Mark 10:45).

Also included are those who have a negative influence on me, sometimes through no fault of their own. People whose lifestyle causes me jealousy. People who highlight my insecurity. People whose critical spirit is contagious. People whose core values are in conflict with mine.

Again, these need not automatically be deleted from my life. In many cases, the drain from these relationships is the result of my own emotional and spiritual immaturity. If someone makes me feel insecure, I'm not really comprehending my identity in Jesus Christ, because it is only that relationship which can ultimately define my worth. God can use even those relationships that cause me anxiety to refine me.

Energizing Relationships

I have been the recipient of some rich friendships. Merle Mees, a friend in Kansas, calls several times a year just to ask what books I've been reading and to recommend a few he's read that have helped him grow. I inevitably read the books he recommends, and I can't remember a time his advice didn't enrich me.

My wife Susan believes in me so strongly that I strive to become the man she believes me to be. My senior pastor and preaching partner, Rick White, has set a lofty standard for biblical teaching within our church; therefore, I preach better at home than anywhere else.

Then there are other relationships that are just pure pleasure. I've noticed that those who most energize me are incredibly funny. People who make me laugh restore my spirit quicker than any other kind of people. When things get too hectic, Susan will tell me, "You need to spend a day fishing with Bill." By the time Bill and I arrive at the river, I'm already energized from laughing. My daughters are both naturally funny. Time spent with them, with no particular agenda, always picks me up.

Get around people who have something of value to share with you. Find a wise elder to mentor you. A child to invest in. A person in need to share with. A friend with whom to laugh and cry. Their impact will continue to have a significant effect on your life long after they have departed.

Now What?

Once we have identified the relational drains and inlets into our lives, it's time for an evaluation. Sometimes we discover that we are being blessed by many people, but we are hard pressed to find people into whom we are pouring our lives. That's a clear mandate to find someone to serve.

More frequently, we discover our relational income is insufficient to keep up with our relational output. We have two options—find more people to pour into us and begin to cut back on what we are giving. The first makes sense. The second causes some people to feel uncomfortable. How do we turn away people who need us?

Is this ever a legitimate option for the Christ-follower? Are we ever justified in turning away people who need us? Is that being selfish? It could be. But Jesus himself taught the value of retreating from demanding people at times. Jesus sent his disciples out on their first mission without him. "They went out and preached that people should repent. They drove out many demons and anointed many sick people with oil and healed them" (Mark 6:12–13). While they were away, Jesus received tragic news. His cousin and spiritual forerunner, John the Baptizer, had been killed by King Herod.

When the disciples returned to their grieving Master, they were jubilant but exhausted. They gave a report. "The apostles gathered around Jesus and reported to him all they had done and taught. Then, because so many people were coming and going that they did not even have a chance to eat, he said to them, 'Come with me by yourselves to a quiet place and get some rest'" (v. 30–31).

What happened when they arrived at that quiet place kept them from retreating immediately. A crowd gathered, hungry for Jesus' teaching. "When Jesus landed and saw a large crowd, he had compassion on them, because they were like sheep without a shepherd. So he began teaching them many things" (v. 34).

That was the occasion for one of Jesus' most spectacular miracles—the feeding of over five thousand people with just a kid's sack lunch. While the crowd was finishing their meal, Jesus sent the disciples to Bethsaida. "After leaving them, he went up on a mountainside to pray" (v. 46).

Clearly, there are times to retreat, even when demands on us from others are high.

Drawing Some Boundaries

To be effective some of the time, we cannot be accessible all of the time.

Sometimes it a matter of managing time spent with people. There are some people you can afford to spend a few minutes with, but not a few hours. We have the most flexibility in balancing our relationships outside of work. We don't have as much choice about who we must interact with on the job. But even in that context, we can learn to manage the drains on our emotional reserves.

Meetings. Set the example by carefully considering who really needs to attend your meeting. Question every invitation to attend a meeting by asking, "Why do you need me to attend?" It's amazing how frequently people can't give a clear answer. By bargaining for a five-minute overview after the meeting, you can redeem valuable time for more important projects.

Phone calls. For some, answering the phone *is* their job. For others, it is a distraction. There are times I set my phone to go directly to voice mail. Otherwise, I would be repeatedly interrupted from other important things I'm working on. Yet if I get a voice mail or phone call from someone in need, I must be able to put other things aside and minister to that person right then. The phone makes a great tool but a ruthless master.

E-mail. What did we do at work before E-mail? I could fill a forty-hour week with just this one means of communication, often getting fifty or more a day. Much of the E-mail I get every day is the equivalent of junk mail. The sooner it's deleted, the better. Another big chunk of mail is sent "FYI"—things I need to know about but don't need to act on. Only a small percentage requires me to respond in some way. Unless I'm expecting something urgent, I check my E-mail first thing in the morning, after lunch, then again before I leave for the day—if I have time.

People. This is the most difficult area for anyone to manage, especially someone in ministry. At times I don't mind being distracted, such as when I'm doing work that doesn't require sustained concentration. At other times I prefer not to be interrupted, but I am happy to take interruptions if they are important. Sometimes though, I'm concentrating on a difficult project or a complex passage of Scripture, and I don't want to be distracted unless the building is on fire.

Some people are my business; others keep me from my business. It's important to know the difference. Drop-in visitors can waste a lot of time. Colleagues who stop by just to chat for long periods of time, assistants needing help on small matters that can wait, or sales representatives who slip past the receptionist can keep me from working on a message that will impact a lot of people next Sunday.

With these types of interruptions, I've found a way to prevent a casual visit from taking me away from the task at hand. If someone needs a quick word, I stand up. This allows them to get straight to the point, allows me to help them, and gets us both back to our tasks in the minimum amount of time. If I see it is a matter that will take some time, I either suggest another time to talk or offer the person a chair and put my agenda to the side for the time being.

In some environments, you may have the option of refusing to accept interruption without an appointment. If someone else's crisis took weeks, even years to develop, waiting until tomorrow or the next day to discuss it likely won't make a difference. In my situation, however, I've found that it often takes a lot of emotional energy for a person in crisis to come see me, so I don't want to put them off if at all possible.

Keep a prayerful attitude about every relationship. Some of the people I most enjoy being with can be slowly but subtly destroying my attitude. Likewise, God has used some of my most difficult relationships to break my selfish pride and strong will. Asking God for discernment and insight is a prayer that I seldom offer without seeing results.

In summary, it's mostly a matter of paying attention. Other people will be a primary means by which God does his work in me. And I will be a tool in his hands for shaping the character of others. I do a better job of managing the inlet and output of my emotional assets just by remembering these truths.

CHAPTER NINETEEN

Winners Know the Difference
Between a Rut and a Routine

*Be patient, then, brothers, until the Lord's coming. See how the
farmer waits for the land to yield its valuable crop and how
patient he is for the autumn and spring rains. You too, be patient
and stand firm, because the Lord's coming is near.*
—James 5:7–8

ROUTINES HAVE A BAD REPUTATION. Some people think a routine
and a rut are the same thing, but there is a world of difference.
A rut is a mindless recycling of yesterday, doing the same thing
over and over, without any thought of why or why not. A routine may consist of doing the same thing over and over again,
but the repetition is intentional, with a specific goal in mind.

Investing a few dollars wisely every payday is not a glam-
orous way to wealth, but it is certainly one of the most dependable. Walking the dog for thirty minutes each morning may not
be a competitive sport, but it's a great way to keep healthy and
welcome the world each day. Writing a few notes of encouragement each week may not win you a Pulitzer Prize, but it will
yield rich relational rewards in the years to come.

Sometimes, though, people who are seeking success in life
overlook routine in their desire to change the world. We had
rather start something new than maintain something already
established.

It is easier for many people to get excited about building a
new house than about maintaining one. We live in an older
home, and several of the windowsills are beginning to show the

results of Tennessee's humid weather. The topic of patching and repainting the rotting woodwork came up the other morning. With complete seriousness I grumped, "Maybe we should just think about moving. In fact, we should just build a new house so we don't have all this maintenance."

I won't print my wife's response verbatim; suffice it to say she was quite underwhelmed by the idea. The routine maintenance that comes with home ownership is no fun for me or anyone else, but if I want to keep it from falling in around me, I'd better invest in some routine upkeep on a consistent basis.

What is it in your business that is routine, mundane, ordinary—what would you rather overlook?

Wendy's founder and president, Dave Thomas, said, "A lot of folks today don't like routine. Not me. I'm all for it. Take clean restaurants, for instance. If there ever was a routine that needed following, it's getting a restaurant ready to open for customers every day. As I travel around the country visiting Wendy's restaurants, the managers always know I'm coming. Not surprisingly, a lot of extra effort goes on before I get there to make the restaurants sparkling clean. I'm glad they do it, but I wish I could get every manager to act like I was going to visit their restaurant every day of the year."[21]

It's amazing to see the things people will do to avoid a routine. I have a friend who, about once a year, goes on a crash diet and begins a rigorous fitness program until he loses twenty or so pounds. As soon as he starts feeling better, he reverts to his old habits of eating and inactivity. He can't seem to maintain routine habits of eating right and getting consistent exercise.

I've known sales people who were great at closing a deal, but they left sales because they couldn't maintain the daily routine of finding prospective clients.

I know another man who, several years ago, quit his job and relocated his wife and teenagers in order to attend Bible college. After one semester, he dropped out. He told me one of the reasons he had done this was that it had been difficult for him to read his Bible on a daily basis, so he thought he would go learn it all at once.

As I met and talked with people in their seventies and eighties in preparation for this book, they made life look so simple. A common denominator with all is that they have made time every day for routines that ensure health and personal growth. They did small things well, consistently for a long time, which yielded rich returns.

What are the mundane activities that make for a life well lived?

Going for the Goal

Years ago I learned an important lesson about goal-setting from my friend Charlene Armitage. Charlene is married to my mentor Vernon, whom I've mentioned several times before. Charlene taught a leadership class and encouraged us to use Luke 2:52 as a guide for setting personal goals: "And Jesus grew in wisdom and stature, and in favor with God and men."

Charlene taught, "Life goals are reached by setting annual goals. Annual goals are reached by reaching daily goals. Daily goals are reached by doing things which may be uncomfortable at first but eventually become habits. Habits are powerful things. Habits turn actions into attitudes, and attitudes into lifestyles."

For almost fifteen years now, I've set
- an *intellectual* goal (Jesus grew in wisdom),
- a *physical* goal (in stature),
- a *spiritual* goal (in favor with God), and
- a *relational* goal (in favor with men).

I've set these goals for the following year, usually during the week between Christmas and New Year's Day.

These goals are not spectacular like, "Win the world to Christ in 2002." In fact, they are sometimes rather boring. What I'm attempting to do is to spend a year cultivating a habit in each of these areas. By the time that year is over, I can usually maintain these habits without a lot of energy. Then the next year, I can learn four new *habits* that will lead me toward becoming the man God has called me to be. I don't always completely reach them, but over the past decade and a half, I've grown tremendously, and these "habit goals" are a big reason why.

Spiritual Routines

Evangelicals often use the phrases "daily devotionals" and "quiet time" to refer to a specific time spent in spiritual activities such as reading a devotional guide, prayer, and Bible-reading.

Over the years, I've tried to develop some spiritual routines that have specific purposes. For example, many Christians use a journal—some to keep notes from their study of the Bible, others to keep a record of their lives for posterity. Early in my quest to develop spiritual habits, I started writing my prayers. I can easily get distracted if I pray in the traditional "bow your head and silently converse with God" format. But writing a letter to God each morning allows me to capture my thoughts and be specific in my conversation with him.

I've especially found this helpful in the area of confession. Because journaling is generally a daily discipline, I've incorporated daily confession of sin into my walk. The Bible teaches us to keep short accounts with God, and twenty-four hours is about as long as I can go without forgetting the damaging acts of rebellion and selfish living that keep me from knowing God intimately. I've developed a code, known only to me, so that if ever one of these journals should be read by someone else, at least my most grievous sins will remain a secret between God and me.

Journaling also helps me know if I am practicing acts of repentance and forgiveness. If this morning's journal entry reads much like one from last year, "And Lord, I'm struggling to forgive . . ." then most likely I'm not choosing to forgive but am just giving lip service to this basic requirement. Here are other spiritual routines worth cultivating:

Prayer-walking. As you run, walk, or drive through your neighborhood, pray for each household along the way. Even if you don't know the occupants, God will often use your prayers to open opportunities for evangelism and ministry.

Forgiving immediately. Having learned the hard way how destructive an unforgiving heart can be, I am trying consciously to forgive people who hurt me or anger me at the very moment of their trespass. When I forget, my journal reminds me to do so. Since forgiveness is a choice of the will, not an emotion, I can choose to harbor enmity until it festers, or I can get rid of it immediately.

Finding a spiritual coach. I've been blessed by the opportunity to walk closely with several men who have coached me in the ways of spiritual growth. Prayerfully ask God to lead you to someone who will help you see your blind spots and keep you pointed in the way of the cross.

Physical Routines

When we view exercise as one more thing to be added to our daily routine, it often gets left out. When we view a diet as something to be endured for a season, we see temporary results at best.

Healthy living comes from healthy habits. Healthy habits come when we quit seeking the short-term fix and become more interested in making small but permanent changes we can live with for the long haul. Better health, reduced stress, and greater endurance make finding enjoyable physical activity worth the effort.

My physical goals have been based on the reality that small things done consistently over long periods yield significant results. One year my goal was, "Quit looking for the easy way to get somewhere." At the time I was working on the fourth floor of an office building, so I cultivated the habit of taking the stairs instead of the elevator. I quit looking for the closest parking spot at the grocery store. I quit asking the kids to run up stairs to get something for me and did it myself.

Three days a week I head to the gym for thirty minutes of cardiovascular work followed by thirty minutes of weight-lifting. Another two or three days a week, I run through my neighborhood or in the park. I go whether I feel like it or not, whether I had a good night's sleep or not, whether I've got a busy day or not. I don't schedule breakfast appointments with people. I refuse to break my routine if at all possible.

Why? Because I'm some kind of a fitness nut? No. Because I love the rewards of working out more than I enjoy working out. So on days that I don't particularly feel like exercising, I remind myself of the many benefits I'm receiving: stress reduction, increased stamina for ministry. I make deals with myself, saying, *Go for fifteen minutes. If you still don't feel like running, you can turn around and walk home.* Most of the time, once I get started, I can endure to the end of the workout.

Christians have not always viewed healthy living as a stewardship issue. Those who want to live to the fullest the abundant life Jesus promised will take steps to ensure that they've done all they can to be physically fit.

Intellectual Routines

I collect books the way some kids collect baseball cards. My books aren't rare or valuable to anyone else, but they have been the primary means by which I have grown.

Early in my ministry, I would set a numerical goal such as, "Read twenty-five books this year." Throughout that year, I would read books on church growth, leadership, theology, preaching—along with a few good novels—to reach my goal.

These days, I pick a particular topic for a year and try to read the major body of work written on it. Two years ago, I narrowed my focus from leadership in general to the subject of change and how to lead people in the change process. Last year I read everything I could get my hands on about teamwork. This year I have been studying the subject of worship, both personal and corporate. Limiting my intellectual goal to one particular area has helped me immensely.

I'm also committing to teach particular subjects that I want to know more about. That forces me to study and prepare for something that might remain a wishful thought otherwise.

Relational Routines

A task-oriented guy like me can easily neglect to cultivate relationships. I have always had many friendly acquaintances but few close friendships. In recent years I've grown to value the way God uses people close to me to help me grow into the man I want to become.

Relational goals have allowed me to take small steps toward becoming more people-focused in every area of my life. One year my goal was, "Learn to say 'thank you.'" It was a year-long process of recognizing how many people offer me gifts of their time and energy throughout the day. When the guy at the store sacks my groceries, I try to make eye contact and give an intentional "Thanks." A thank-you note to those who participate in our weekly services conveys heart-felt gratitude for enriching our corporate worship.

A significant part of our success in life will come from the network of relationships that we build over a lifetime. In Romans 16, Paul greeted a number of people (Andronicus, Junias, Ampliatus, Urbanus, and Stachys, just to name a few) that are unknown to us, but were vital extensions of his ministry.

This year I'm working hard to expand my circle of relationships to include people of varied backgrounds. When you are a white, married, middle-class male, chances are good that most of your acquaintances are white, married, middle-class males.

When we allow ourselves to expand our friendships beyond racial, socioeconomic, and other potential barriers, we come away with a richer awareness of life.

Neglect of either intellectual, physical, spiritual, or relational routines will result in disappointment as we look back upon our lives. Knowing we failed to maximize the intelligence God gave us, realizing that our lives have been shortened by neglecting physical development, becoming aware of a stunted spiritual life, or experiencing the loneliness of not having built a strong network of relationships—all of these will keep us from enjoying our later years.

Most people feel good when they accomplish something significant for the first time. But as we become more proficient at something, we often lose that sense of accomplishment. Almost all the habits and attitudes we've examined can become routine. In fact, that's the goal. Good routines lead to good results. Learning to find satisfaction in developing and maintaining good routines helps make the race worth running.

CHAPTER TWENTY

Winners Live a Lifestyle of Celebration

*"But the father said to his servants, 'Quick! Bring the best robe
and put it on him. Put a ring on his finger and sandals on his
feet. Bring the fattened calf and kill it. Let's have a feast and celebrate. For this son of mine was dead and is alive again; he was
lost and is found.' So they began to celebrate."*
—Luke 15:22–24

IT'S A FAMILIAR STORY. Walt and Linda Stuart lived in the same
southern city for over thirty years. Walt worked hard for the
same steel company his entire career, moving up in responsibility and income every few years. The Stuarts built a modest
home and raised three children there, never moving even after
their income improved dramatically. Linda joked about their
frugality, telling friends her job was clipping coupons and saying no to children. They seldom ate out in restaurants, and they
bought cars that other people had worn out. Gifts for Christmas
and birthdays were usually clothing or other necessities.

But their frugality was intentional. Together they dreamed
of an early retirement and the opportunity to travel exten-
sively across the United States. Maps, brochures for motor
homes, and travel magazines were always evident on the coffee table, and they occupied a lot of their discussion. But they
never traveled.

Family vacations consisted of visits to relatives, unless the
rare business trip afforded the opportunity for double duty. "We
can't afford it" was such a common response to their children's

requests for anything pleasurable that one of the daughters, in adulthood, said, "I really thought my folks were poor."

But through careful planning and scrimping, Walt reached his goal of early retirement at age fifty-five. The next day, he and Linda went shopping for motor homes; that night they began plotting out the trip across the United States they had dreamed of for years. The next morning, Walt suffered a massive and fatal heart attack while mowing the grass.

The Stuarts waited to enjoy life until retirement. For Walt, there was no more life to enjoy.

In what was perhaps his most famous parable, Jesus introduced us to three characters—the prodigal son, the father, and an older brother. Jesus told this story as one of three parables in response to an accusation from the religious leaders of his day that "this man welcomes sinners and eats with them."

The father in the story represents God. The prodigal (which means "wasteful") represents those who have made choices that have led them to sin and shame. The older brother represents religious people who dislike "sinners" and are resentful of the Father's love for them.

This parable gives us a lot of insight into the nature of God. After the prodigal son took his share of the inheritance and left the farm, the father spent many hours watching up the road, waiting for the son's return. The son squandered all he had as fast as he could, wasting both his inheritance and his potential, until finally he came to his senses and returned in humility to his father.

The father's (God's) response? "Let's celebrate! (The word appears four times in this passage.) Call the neighbors; it's party time!" Quite a contrast to the response of the older brother, who not only objected that his father would host a party for the returning wanderer but who also by his own admission had never even celebrated lesser events with his friends.

God's nature is to celebrate. A look at the creation narratives in Genesis verifies this. After each day's creative work, God would pause and say, "This is good." Then on the seventh day, when God's creation was completed, he rested and reflected on what he had done.

A look at the Gospels shows that Jesus, God incarnate, had a reputation for being a person who knew how to celebrate. He was not the austere, serious figure associated with so many of the biblical prophets who preceded him. His *joie de vivre* was evident; the ease with which he associated with people who had not yet discovered God's love was a mystery to the religious leaders of his day. His critics called him "a glutton and a drunkard, a friend of tax collectors and 'sinners'" (Luke 7:34). Matthew's Gospel records an example of the type of gathering that led to such accusations.

> While Jesus was having dinner at Matthew's house, many tax collectors and "sinners" came and ate with him and his disciples. When the Pharisees saw this, they asked his disciples, "Why does your teacher eat with tax collectors and 'sinners'?"
>
> On hearing this, Jesus said, "It is not the healthy who need a doctor, but the sick. But go and learn what this means: 'I desire mercy, not sacrifice.' For I have not come to call the righteous, but sinners."
>
> Then John's disciples came and asked him, "How is it that we and the Pharisees fast, but your disciples do not fast?"
>
> Jesus answered, "How can the guests of the bridegroom mourn while he is with them? The time will come when the bridegroom will be taken from them; then they will fast" (Matt. 9:10–15).

Jesus gave the church the ordinances of baptism and communion as opportunities to joyfully remember his gifts to us. He promised us that heaven will be full of opportunities to celebrate, especially when we consider the hope of a future without sin and accusation.

"Then I heard a loud voice in heaven say: 'Now have come the salvation and the power and the kingdom of our God, and the authority of his Christ. For the accuser of our brothers, who accuses them before our God day and night, has been hurled down. They overcame him by the blood of the Lamb and by the word of their testimony; they did not love their lives so much as to shrink from death. Therefore rejoice, you heavens and you who dwell in them!'" (Rev. 12:10–12).

Party-Inhibited

Unfortunately, many otherwise successful people have a difficult time emulating this characteristic of God. People who strive toward success are often highly task-oriented. Such people are more comfortable *doing* than reflecting or celebrating. They may also have perfectionistic tendencies. These very qualities that cause them to be action-oriented and to do their work with excellence also become the inhibitors of celebration and joy in their lives.

It's true that more people struggle with delayed gratification—unable to save a dollar now to spend later or unable to say no to something in order to say yes to something more important. But there are also many who suffer from its polar opposite. Postponing all gratification makes for a dull life and is evidence of a spiritual malady. There is no guarantee of tomorrow. Celebration is a way of ensuring we recognize and appreciate life and all its blessings.

Barriers

Why do some of us put off celebration time and time again? Why do we wait to say "thank you" or "I love you"? Why do we downplay birthdays and anniversaries? Why is it so hard for us to recognize the accomplishments of others?

The primary reason is fear. We are afraid that if we slow down long enough to celebrate, we'll lose momentum. We are afraid that if we praise our employees for their work or our children for their grades, they'll be satisfied with their performance and quit striving for greater excellence. We are afraid that if we turn loose of a few dollars to celebrate now, we'll go into a spending frenzy that won't end until we're destitute and living in a gutter somewhere.

Some people struggle with a fear of appearing boastful or proud. While the current generation has grown up hearing about the importance of our "self-esteem," our parents were often taught, "Don't draw attention to yourself." Theirs may have been the last generation to worry about getting "the big head."

Understanding that celebrating does not have to be the same as boasting is one way to overcome this hurdle. Reaching a major milestone in a career or a pursuit is something to be recognized, and those who love us will want to commemorate that event with us.

Planning a celebration for a family member's or colleague's accomplishment will not give them "the big head," but something better. It will give them a "big heart" full of gratitude and the motivation to continue to pursue excellence.

When a husband plans an anniversary celebration—flowers, a card, dinner at her favorite restaurant, taking care of childcare arrangements—his investment of time in working out these details will be recognized and far more valued by his wife than the details or gifts themselves.

When a parent takes time to prepare a favorite meal for her child who has just finished fourth grade, or completed a piano recital, or won the Little League championship, or scored well on college entrance exams, it says to that child, "What's important to you is important to all of us."

Benefits

Few things reinforce family ties more than celebrating together the blessings of life. Our oldest daughter had a role in the Christmas musical produced by our church's children's ministry when she was ten. She did a wonderful job. After the service, we gave her a bouquet of flowers and went home for one of her favorite desserts. That night gave me an odd feeling of being both in the present and in the future. I could almost see us, twenty years from now, seated around that same table, reminiscing about that night.

Celebration makes us slow down long enough to reflect. Reflection, for the Christian, should lead to a sense of thanksgiving. Busy people often overlook God's blessings. Living with a sense of gratitude is essential for anyone who desires to know contentment and satisfaction in life. In fact, one of the reasons some people never seem to find satisfaction is their inability to stop long enough to rest in their current achievements.

Ingredients for Celebration

People who matter to you. A friend once gave me some wise advice: "Never have a pity party. The food's lousy and the fun people never show up." But fun people will come to a celebration. Learning to share important events with others is the key to cementing those memories. When we reach the home stretch of life, to be able to reminisce with loved ones about vacations, parties, and special events is one of life's great pleasures.

Something that will acknowledge the significance of the event. A person doesn't need to be an expert photographer to capture special events on film, thanks to today's point-and-shoot technology. I have a friend who films baptisms in our church with his camcorder. Then he gives the tape to the person who was baptized.

We frequently give a plaque or some kind of memento to people as a way of saying "thank you" or to signify an anniversary or an award of some kind. I've received several such plaques for different things, and I appreciate the spirit behind all of them. On the wall behind me, for example, I have a couple of plaques from the YMCA—gestures of thanks for coaching girls' basketball.

But my greatest treasure from coaching is a basketball signed by all the girls in their own handwriting. Why? It's more personal. Just underneath my diplomas from seminary and college, I have a framed, handmade certificate declaring me "Best Dad in the Universe!"

A pastor friend recently moved to another church. The congregation he had served for eight years held a wonderful reception to honor his ministry there. He received not a plaque but a book containing handwritten letters from people in his congregation thanking him for specific times he had ministered to them, sermons they remembered, and funny events that had occurred in the life of the church while he had served there.

Celebration does not have to mean spending a lot of money. Although giving an expensive gift is the easiest thing to do, a handwritten note or photograph may be the most memorable remembrance we can give.

Celebrations come in all sizes and shapes. Spur-of-the-moment events will flow just as easily as major events when our heart is calibrated to celebration. The magnitude of the celebration is in proportion to the significance of the event.

Celebrate for important reasons. Weddings, milestone wedding anniversaries, promotions, graduations, births of children and grandchildren, a family member coming to Christ—these are all major life events that are worthy of remembering with a party of some kind. But just as valid are celebrations for the smallest reason. A good report card, an unexpected windfall, encouraging test results from the doctor's office—all these can become the catalyst for celebration.

The first day that feels like spring will find me doing busy-work out in the garden. It's still too early to plant, but the warm sun on my face is like medicine for my soul after too much time indoors. Conversely, the first day I feel that cool, dry wind of autumn makes me celebrate the end of another long, hot summer. God's cycle of the seasons becomes another reason to gratefully celebrate his provisions.

Celebration as Worship

Celebrating can also be an act of worship, a way to acknowledge God's blessings. When God set up his covenantal relationship with those former Egyptian slaves who became the nation of Israel, he instituted a series of celebrations, each designed to help people remember the goodness of God and his provision, both past and future. There were daily, weekly, monthly, and yearly festivals, and proper observance of them was required.

Two examples are the Sabbath and the Passover. The Sabbath was a gift of one day each week for God's people to rest from the back-breaking labor of subsistence living and to reflect on God's blessings. The Passover feast was given to celebrate their deliverance from Egyptian slavery and the Exodus, which would eventually lead them into the home God had prepared for them.

Our definition of worship needs to be big enough to include not only reverence and devotion but also acknowledgment of the infinite reasons to celebrate God's love and devotion to his children.

A Future to Be Avoided

I've glimpsed the future—an old man, gruff and distant from those who love him, heart rusted shut from disuse. All around him are those who love him, children and grandchildren, gathered to celebrate his birthday. But he's not having any of it. His inability to participate causes pain, both to those assembled and to himself. In his drive to achieve, he neglected to celebrate. Like a muscle that was never used, his capacity to enjoy life has withered away to nothing. Those who love him think it is their fault, that their efforts to honor him aren't good enough or appropriate. He can no more articulate his handicap than an ostrich can tell you why it can't fly. Stunted, he sits in his chair, not even aware of how desperately he wants to loosen up and join the fun.

I know that man, at least who he was. And I'm determined to make sure he never is.

CHAPTER TWENTY-ONE

Winners Have Learned to Manage Discomfort

Endure hardship as discipline.
—Hebrews 12:7

I'VE RUN FOR THE BETTER PART OF TWENTY YEARS NOW. In my twenties, I ran daily, up to sixty miles in a week when preparing for a marathon. I participated in 10K races just about every weekend and pursued no other hobbies.

Today, I run just three or four days a week, for about thirty minutes at a stretch. I'm slower, and I run now more for the health benefits than the competition. If I race, I'm just as likely to run with a friend for fun as to go all out. I don't even think of running as a hobby anymore; it's just something I do. But one thing hasn't changed. Running still hurts.

Don't misunderstand. I love to run. I love the release from stress it gives me. I love how being healthy makes me feel younger than my years. I love running at the crack of dawn in sultry summer. I love braving the elements in winter. I love running beneath the blossoming trees in spring and their brilliant leaves in fall. But running hurts.

I'm not talking about the pain of injuries. I have enough sense to stop running if I need to in order to heal from a running-related injury. The hurt I'm talking about is vague and hard to describe.

After logging thousands of miles, I still come to a point, about a mile into just about every run, when I think, *This is too uncomfortable. I should give this up.* But I seldom do. I persevere.

Often the discomfort eases—and sometimes the whole run is miserable. Yet I never regret running when I'm done.

When I started running, I thought a day would come when I would have a breakthrough, and suddenly running would be an effortless and blissful experience. I had been at it for over a year when my running mentor told me the hard truth. Larry Lewis, a veteran by that time of over twenty marathons, said simply, "It's always going to hurt. Get used to it. Distance running is the art of managing discomfort."

Philosophers and preachers have come up with a thousand metaphors for life, but my favorite is the apostle Paul's depiction of life as a race to be won. Running was his favorite example of persevering in the faith. Consider the following:

> However, I consider my life worth nothing to me, if only I may finish the race and complete the task the Lord Jesus has given me—the task of testifying to the gospel of God's grace (Acts 20:24).

> Do you not know that in a race all the runners run, but only one gets the prize? Run in such a way as to get the prize. Everyone who competes in the games goes into strict training. They do it to get a crown that will not last; but we do it to get a crown that will last forever. Therefore I do not run like a man running aimlessly; I do not fight like a man beating the air. No, I beat my body and make it my slave so that after I have preached to others, I myself will not be disqualified for the prize (1 Cor. 9:24–27).

> I went in response to a revelation and set before them the gospel that I preach among the Gentiles. But I did this privately to those who seemed to be leaders, for fear that I was running or had run my race in vain (Gal. 2:2).

You were running a good race. Who cut in on you and kept you from obeying the truth? (Gal. 5:7).

I have fought the good fight, I have finished the race, I have kept the faith (2 Tim. 4:7).

Do everything without complaining or arguing, so that you may become blameless and pure, children of God without fault in a crooked and depraved generation, in which you shine like stars in the universe as you hold out the word of life—in order that I may boast on the day of Christ that I did not run or labor for nothing (Phil. 2:14–16).

Not that I have already obtained all this, or have already been made perfect, but I press on to take hold of that for which Christ Jesus took hold of me. Brothers, I do not consider myself yet to have taken hold of it. But one thing I do: Forgetting what is behind and straining toward what is ahead, I press on toward the goal to win the prize for which God has called me heavenward in Christ Jesus (Phil. 3:12–14).

The writer of Hebrews 12:1–3 picked up the imagery as well: "Therefore, since we are surrounded by such a great cloud of witnesses, let us throw off everything that hinders and the sin that so easily entangles, and let us run with perseverance the race marked out for us. Let us fix our eyes on Jesus, the author and perfecter of our faith, who for the joy set before him endured the cross, scorning its shame, and sat down at the right hand of the throne of God. Consider him who endured such opposition from sinful men, so that you will not grow weary and lose heart."

Verses like these were at the heart of my desire to write this book. Running has been an important part of my life for over

twenty years now. I've learned some valuable lessons about finishing well from lacing up my shoes and hitting the pavement.

A Defining Race

As we stood at the starting line that cold, rainy October
morning in 1983, more than a few of the four thousand people
gathered were wondering why we would ever want to run 26.2
miles in the first place, much less spend a quarter of a year training for it. Then the starting gun fired, and we started moving
through the streets of Kansas City, Missouri.

I had been up since 4:00 that morning, driving sixty miles
with my running partners for what we all hoped would be a race
for our personal best. I had completed four marathons prior to
this event, so I wasn't concerned about covering the distance. I
had a specific goal in mind: to finish under three hours and ten
minutes. This was nine minutes faster than I had ever run the
race before, but my hope was to qualify for the Boston
Marathon, then the most prestigious road race in the country.

That meant I had to maintain an average pace of just less
than seven and one-half minutes per mile. I had followed a
detailed training program that gave me confidence that I could
handle the pace and the distance, hitting every benchmark in
the process. I had been healthy throughout the training process,
something I couldn't say about other races where I had often
worked through injury and illness. This looked like my day.

The temperature was in the 50s, cool for spectators, ideal for
distance running because it slowed the dehydration that plagues
hot-weather runners. The light drizzle was uncomfortable but
not problematic as long as we kept moving.

That was my problem—I was struggling to keep moving. I
was covering ground but laboring far more than I expected to so
early in the race. I played all the mind games I used to keep
myself going on long practice runs, but I was beginning to wonder if I would even finish, much less meet my goal. I had no
physical pain, just an indefinable sense of dread at the prospect
of finishing.

I stopped to walk for the first time around mile twelve, less than halfway through the race. Not a good sign. After a hundred yards or so, I began to run again, but a degenerating cycle set in. I would run a short while, then walk. Run and walk. As a result of the decreased effort, the rain began to chill me. Around mile eighteen, I quit running altogether and trudged on in an icy fog of despondency.

The race organizers had made safety a priority; as a result, a number of vehicles were patrolling the course, picking up the injured and ill prepared, wrapping them in blankets, and delivering them to the area beyond the finish line where the finishers were celebrating.

Twice one of these rescue vehicles stopped and asked me if I wanted a ride; I ignored them and started jogging until they were out of sight. I was not yet able to concede that the race was already over for me.

By the third time a rescue vehicle pulled alongside, I was beginning to shiver uncontrollably, probably in the early stages of hypothermia. I shook my head when the young woman on the passenger's side asked if I needed help. Assessing my condition, she said, "We've got warm blankets and hot chocolate."

My last bit of resolve evaporated, and I got into the van, where I immediately burst into tears. The blanket and the hot chocolate began to warm my body, but my mood was still cold. I had failed to finish. I had not met my goal.

When I found my friends, they were glad to see me and immediately wanted to know my time. My shame intensified as I told them what happened. They all tried to console me, but they knew the scope of my disappointment. Thankfully, they refrained from saying, "At least you tried." They knew that was the last thing I wanted to hear. They were even guarded about talking of their own well-run race in front of me.

I eventually recovered from that disappointment, but I have never attempted another marathon. I've often wondered why that event from so many years ago became such a defining moment in my life. There was no Olympic medal on the line, no prize money. My friends and family still loved me just as much after as they did before the race. No one else was harmed as a result of my failure that day. Why did that failure hurt so much?

I believe it was because my failure was an emotional lapse, not a physical one. Although I had endured many long, painful training runs and races in the past, on that day I couldn't manage my discomfort.

As a pastor, I've heard a lot of people say, "Life is hard." I always want to reply, "Compared to what?" But I rein in my sarcasm and ask why they make that statement. They'll go on to reveal a broken marriage, troubled job situation, financial struggles, or a broken heart. They are experiencing the reality that life can be uncomfortable, even miserable, at times.

We've all been through periods when we said, "I just feel like giving up." A young mother I know well, after a bad day of dealing with the most strong-willed little girl imaginable said, "Where do I go to resign?" Some have dealt with situations so painful for so long that their desire to quit leads them to consider suicide.

Short of that irreversible option, people find all kinds of ways to give up. There are marriages where neither spouse has been emotionally involved for decades. Parents have given up on their teenagers because they can't take the inevitable confrontation necessary to keep their child on track in this valueless age.

Thousands of workers across the country are killing time, emotionally absent from their work, doing just enough to get by, not even hoping anymore that work will be meaningful again some day.

Artists, musicians, and writers have put their brushes and instruments and pens away. They have given up their dream, given up their passion to hone their craft, and resigned themselves to a job they hate as a means of paying the bills and getting through life without any more disappointment.

Congregations are going through the motions each Sunday, unwilling to move beyond their comfort level in order to reach people with the gospel.

In all of these examples, we see that giving up when life hurts is the surest way to ensure a meaningless existence.

Moving Beyond Comfort

If anyone had a reason to give up, it would have been Lance Armstrong. Lance was a world-class cyclist, one of the rare Americans competing in the elite road races of Europe.

In 1996, the twenty-four-year-old climbed to the number-one ranking in his sport but was then diagnosed with testicular cancer. The cancer had metastasized and spread to his lungs and brain. Few expected him to survive the disease.

Yet in the summer of 1999, Armstrong not only recovered from the cancer but even went on to win the most prestigious race in cycling, the Tour de France. Cynics called it a fluke, because some of the best cyclists sat out the race due to a doping scandal. Few believed he would win in the year 2000, when the best cyclists would be back and the course would be more mountainous. But he not only won in 2000, he won by a whopping six minutes!

In interviews and a best-selling book *It's Not About the Bike: My Journey Back to Life*, Armstrong has repeatedly stated that what had been his greatest adversary, the cancer, became his advantage. After recovering from cancer, Lance was forty pounds lighter. While he bulked up some in the recovery years, he has remained leaner than ever before. This weight loss made a difference in Armstrong's biking and played significantly into his becoming a three-time Tour de France winner.

Think of Lance Armstrong next time you catch yourself whining that "life is hard."

Happiness Is Overrated

If happiness each day is our primary goal, then we naturally reject all experiences that hurt. We avoid situations where we can grow. We rebuff risk and turn away from trials at every opportunity.

A goal of happiness leads to resulting weakness. Happiness is mostly an illusion, and it is highly overrated. I'll go for satisfaction over a job well done any day.

Managing the Discomfort of Change

Habits and attitudes take time—sometimes a long time—to become ingrained within us. Learning new skills is uncomfortable and awkward. Few right-handers would voluntarily learn to write with their left hand. It feels funny and the results are laughable. But if any of us were to lose that hand in an accident, we would quickly adapt.

The only way to make changes that last is to have a compelling motivation. My motivation for change comes from assessing honestly whether my current lifestyle will yield the outcome I desire. It is my desire to live and die being the best Ed Rowell I can be that allows me to manage the discomfort of change.

As I've told people the story of the marathon I didn't finish, some have asked, "Why don't you run another one to make up for your failure? You should get back on the horse that threw you."

For years, I thought that was the thing to do, and I postponed it because the prospect was too painful. I may run another marathon some day, but if and when I do, I'll be free of any sense of trying to redeem myself, because I can now see that failure in perspective.

That failure to finish taught me one of life's most important lessons: *The pain of dropping out will linger long after the pain of perseverance has passed.*

The same applies to life. If you've dropped out of life, it's *never* too late to jump back in. Begin to regain your focus by remembering your life's purpose just for *today*. Regain your self-discipline by postponing immediate gratification just for *today*. Restore a relationship by taking steps toward resolution *today*. Learn to turn off the autopilot of your life when you chart a course of action *today*.

And here's the good news: You'll finish well some day if you finish well each day.

If your race through life finished well today, go to bed with a gratified heart. If not, live purposefully tomorrow. Make the same decision the next day and the next. You are on your way.

You've already got many of these habits and attitudes in place. No one will pick up this book and find all twenty-one habits and attitudes missing from his life. But everyone should find a few that aren't yet in place. Focus on the ones that are weak, and make them your strengths. Let God's unconditional love continually wash away any sense of living so as to earn his favor. And learn to savor the satisfaction of finishing each day well.

That's what I'm doing. I'm nowhere near done yet. But I'm working hard to stay on the course and keep moving. I hope you are doing the same. Live purposely. Finish well. And I'll see you at the finish line.

Conclusion

ANOTHER AUTHOR RECENTLY TOLD ME that finishing a book is a lot like raising a teenager. When they leave home, at first you think you are finished. You congratulate yourself and celebrate the great work you have done. But it isn't long until you see evidence that you might not have done all you could have done.

When that young adult heads out on her own, you are no longer there to take the edge off of life's hardships for her. You won't have the opportunity to discuss all her choices with her, choices that may have serious repercussions. She increasingly forms an identity that doesn't include her parents. Others may never see what you see in her or see what you have strived to instill in her. Only after she is gone will we see areas in which we could have done a better job or given her much-needed skills or confidence.

Once this book is typeset and bound, it will achieve a permanence that makes me uncomfortable. If I have left something unsaid—or worse, said something I didn't intend to say—it will be hard for me to get to every bookstore in the country and use my red pen to write in the margins what I intended to say!

All of us make decisions that will stand long after we have grown to a better understanding of the situation. All of us have made a decision that felt right at the time yet later proved to be wrong. We chide ourselves at such moments, saying, *How could I have made such a stupid decision?* The truth is, it wasn't stupid at all. We made the best choice we could, given what we knew at the time. The fact that we now have information that we didn't have then just means that we are continually learning and growing.

But I do feel confident that the heart of this book will endure. Success is discovering what God has called you to do and to be, then removing any barriers that keep you from experiencing that preferred future. Perhaps you will discover a barrier that I haven't even touched on here. The fact that you have trained yourself to identify your own barriers will be an encouragement to me.

For all who follow Christ, I urge you to seek his best for your life and pursue it no matter what the cost. No other definition of success will provide so rich a reward as hearing someday, "Well done, good and faithful servant."

Notes

1. Quote from Robbie Gordon on speednet.starnews.com, *Indiana Star* online.

2. Henry Blackaby, *Experiencing God* (Nashville: Broadman & Holman, 1998), 28.

3. Kevin and Karen Miller, *More Than You and Me* (Colorado Springs: Focus on the Family Publishing, 1994), 46.

4. "Sinking of the Titanic," *USA Today*, 9 April 1997.

5. Bill Gaither with Jerry Jenkins, *I Almost Missed the Sunset: My Perspectives on Life and Music* (Nashville: Thomas Nelson, 1992), 17–19.

6. James A. Belasco and Ralph C. Stayer, *Flight of the Buffalo* (New York: Warner Books, 1993), 20.

7. Peter Krass, ed., *The Book of Leadership Wisdom: Classic Writings by Legendary Business Leaders* (New York: John Wiley and Sons, 1998), 326.

8. Charlotte Foltz Jones, *Mistakes That Worked* (New York: Doubleday, 1991), 71–72.

9. Seth Godin, "Gear Shops Are No Longer the Engine of Our Economy," *Fast Company*, October 2000, 326.

10. Bud Greenspan, *100 Greatest Moments in Olympic History* (Los Angeles: General Publishing Group, 1995), 98.

11. From an article in *Today's Christian Woman*, July–August 1992, 19.

12. Charlotte Foltz Jones, *Mistakes That Worked* (New York: Doubleday, 1991), 68.

13. Michael Gelb, *How to Think like Leonardo da Vinci* (New York: DTP, 1998), 59.

14. "Stories for Preachers and Teachers," *Media Management*, April 1994, 4.

15. Quoted in Tennessean News Service, 17 April 1998.

16. John Piper, *Desiring God* (Sisters, Oreg.: Multnomah, 1998), 10–11.

17. Quoted in an Internet ad for Roadrunner Sports, 3 October 2000.

18. Quoted in *Time* magazine, 24 April 2000, 76.

19. Quote by Andy Stanley in INJOY's Catalyst Conference for Young Leaders, 19 November 2000.

20. From Mark Hyman's article in *Dad's Magazine*, June 3 2000, 66.

21. Dave Thomas, "The Wonder of Routine," in *The Book of Leadership Wisdom: Classic Writings by Legendary Business Leaders*, ed. Peter Krass (New York: John Wiley and Sons, 1998), 311.